I, An Author

Nicholas Craig has been called everything from 'The Blowtorch of the Barbican' to 'The Uncrowned Vesuvius of the English Classical Stage'. Audiences the world over know Craig the high-octane performer, but in this substantially expanded and updated version of his landmark autobiography we have the very essence of Craig the man: his inner thoughts, his politics, his grievances, his charming house in Richmond.

Lavishly illustrated with yet more photographs of himself, there has never been a more disturbing look into an actor's psyche nor a more penetrating analysis of the craft of acting; from Shakespeare to shouting in restaurants, from corporate videos to station announcements, from Pirandello to making funny noises, to dressing up as a football team mascot and running around at half-time . . .

Nicholas Craig's work since the publication of the first edition of *I, An Actor* has garnered resplendent accolade upon lustrous encomium. The controversial play *Fist F***ing* brought new notoriety and several visits from the Health and Safety officer, and his bravura portrayal of Ebenezer Tumblewhiskers caused many critics to completely revise their views on television costume drama. But the role that introduced him to the widest audience yet, as well as paying for a new kitchen and much-needed overhaul of his central heating system, was Beekar, the evil King of the Thargons in *Gallacticus 439* ('complete tosh of course but immense fun'). The role required him to wear a large striped horn and an ear bobbing on the end of a stalk attached to his nose. He carried it off magnificently and indeed, thus attired, was for a time much in demand as a speaker at sci-fi conventions.

Giddy triumphs notwithstanding, Craig takes no prisoners in his lacerating condemnation of the way he is sometimes treated by commissionaires, BBC Artists' Payments clerks, and younger directors who are often culpably unfamiliar with his previous stage work. His oft-repeated assertion that 'It really is unbefuckinglievable now' might lead one to suppose Craig is becoming cynical as he approaches his middle years but nothing could be further from the truth. A planned sequel to *Gallacticus 439*, a part in *The Bill* and the possibility of a return to the Royal National Theatre for a prestigious revival of the musical *Dames, Dames, Dames!* are reasons enough for Craig to face the future with irrepressible optimism, albeit tinged with a hint of bitterness allied to his unique ability to delight in even the smallest misfortunes of his colleagues.

By the time you have finished this book it is unlikely that you will ever want to read another word written by an actor again.

Nicholas Craig

I, An Actor

---

with Christopher Douglas
and Nigel Planer

Methuen

1 3 5 7 9 10 8 6 4 2

First published in Great Britain in 1988 by Pavilion Books Ltd

This revised edition published 2001 by Methuen Publishing Ltd
215 Vauxhall Bridge Rd, London SW1V 1EJ

Methuen Publishing Limited Reg. No. 3543167

A CIP catalogue record for this book is available from the British Library

ISBN 0 413 76550 4

Designed by Helen Ewing

Printed and bound in Great Britain by
St Edmundsbury Press, Bury St Edmunds, Suffolk

Publishers' note
The majority of the photographs which appear in this autobiography are from the
author's private collection. The publishers are particularly grateful to Nobby Clark for
his special photographic contribution. Other photographs which appear in this book are
reproduced by the kind permission of John Stoddart, Han Lee de Boer, Zoe Dominic,
John Haynes, Donald Cooper, Roy Moseley, Fatimah Namdar, Photosource Limited,
BBC Enterprises Limited, John Timbers and Universal Pictorial Press. Every attempt has
been made to trace copyright holders. We apologize for any omissions and request that
copyright holders contact us at the address above.

An apology

Christopher Douglas and Nigel Planer would like to point out that the characters in this
book are totally fictitious and the events reported entirely untrue. Nicholas Craig's
comments on his fellow professionals are intended in jest. If his remarks appear to be
disloyal, vindictive, bitter, scandalous, insulting or cruel, the reader is asked to bear in
mind that Craig is a disappointed and in many ways a sad man.

Dedication

To Stagehands Everywhere

Contents

Foreword to the 2001 Edition

I was chuffed to the very cockles of my bollocks when Methuen asked me to write a foreword to this latest edition of *I, An Actor* . . . But now that I'm actually faced with the prospect of having to add something sensible to what is rather alarmingly regarded as a classic text, I find myself in a state of complete cerebral meltdown. I'd rather be burnt at the stake than be caught gilding a lily, and as I sit in my dressing room desperately wrestling with my recalcitrant synapses – as well as with these wretched moustache curling-tongs for this evening's performance – I am suddenly seized by a desire to be the sort of person who works in Woolworth's on the Isle of Man and doesn't have to face such absurd challenges. But try I must and fingers to keyboard I will attempt to put, if only for the sake of my splendiferous new publishers, who already seem a lot more helpful than their predecessors – all of whom deservedly lost their jobs shortly after the first edition of *I, An Actor* came out.

How immeasurably different is the process of literary creation nowadays. Yesteryear's pot of biros has been despatched from my dressing table, gone too the scissors and Pritt stick of old, and in their place sits a sleekly winking laptop. Instead of a pile of old script pages, blank sides up, awaiting the press of my Bic, the trusty software thrums behind its little portal. *Actorite 2000* is an ingenious programme that automatically changes fonts and suggests new topics every thirty seconds so you don't get bored or stuck. It was specifically developed for Equity members, but whether it will prove to be the miracle its makers claim remains to be seen. Would *The Duchess of Malfi* have been a greater work if Webster had written it on *Word*? What about *Dandy Dick* on a Dell? A different *kind* of play perhaps, but 'better'. . .? What a profoundly unsettling train of thought. But then what is an actor's mind if not a repository for dark, unspoken fears?

I well remember the feeling of blue-blind, screaming bloody terror when I first sat down to write this damn 'classic' thirteen years ago. Yet even as the waves of nauseous dread came crashing over me I somehow knew it was all there – random thoughts, jottings, a record of my dreams, recipes, snatches of verse, even an idea for a children's book which, by the way, I still think would be an absolute winner with the right illustrator – and not just as a Christmas book either because it's the sort of project one could very easily take to Disney, although they seem only to be interested in unmitigated dross these days. Don't misunderstand me, I think Harry Potter is fab but Sammy the Supermarket Trolley is just that bit more savvy and street sassy, plus he's got a girlfriend (Samantha) with eyelashes on the front of her basket. I've got a bit lost here but the point I was trying to make is that just because someone is able to concentrate their mind to write trenchantly about the craft of acting once, it doesn't necessarily mean they can do it a second time. I'm discovering that writing, like acting, just gets tougher and harder and scarier the more one does it.

In the thirteen years since I performed open heart surgery on myself to produce this book a very, very great deal has happened. Some of it, I have to say, has not been an improvement. I am appalled by the recent cult of celebrity; the way the media endlessly regurgitate the half-baked, 'ecologically-correct' views of assorted supermodels, Spice persons and anyone who's been in a soap for five minutes – it makes me vomit all over my shoes, to be frank. The ill-thought-out, rambling opinions of these class A nonentities might possibly be of use if recycled into toilet paper but not otherwise. I am also incandescent about the way multi-national corporations now control our lives; my dearest wish is to punch one of these conglomerate bosses in the face while screaming 'That's for the polar ice cap. And here's another for the emerging nations!' BIFF! (or whatever the correct onomatopoeia is for the sound of splintering mogul's cranium).

It looks as though the desperate state of the world at the start of the third millennium has serendipitously provided me with a theme for this introduction. Deeply grateful though I am for such a gift from the gods, I am also soul-sick about its implications for the future and, more importantly, for the future of our children. As a multiple Godparent, this is something that concerns me very deeply.

Who, apart from the acting profession and a handful of anti-capitalist demonstrators, is actually *doing* anything about the crisis? On my last birthday, I took my fifteen God-nippers on their annual treat to *Planet Hollywood*. I always do it that way round because if I tried to remember each of their birthdays I would spend my every waking moment shopping in the *Early Learning Centre*. I firmly believe in teaching through play and while we waited for our food to arrive I was doing some impressions of endangered species – a rare parrot and a Madagascan sea cow, as I recall. And do you know they were so unaware of these creatures' plight that all they could say was 'Uncle Nicholas, please stop making that embarrassing noise and put your shoes back on.' So in educational terms we still have an absolute mountain to climb.

Ignorance in the young is perhaps not so very surprising considering the ever lower priority given by the media to anything informative, educational or even grammatically correct. Let's face it, half the people on television aren't even actors – they are gardeners or politicians or newsreaders, not one of whom appears to be able to pronounce the letter 'r', and many of whom employ a system of vowels of no known geographical provenance. Received Pronunciation has been abandoned in favour of a form of English that derives not so much from the estuary as from the sewage works on its banks. I recently had a voicemail from a girl at the publishers saying 'I'm sure once you've managed to marshal your thoughts, Nicholas, we'll have a *rah-ly gerd berk'*. Translation please. If you come across anyone in the media who's actually had a RADA or Webber Douglas voice training you are likely to faint with amazement and have a total conniption.

SCENE: INTERIOR. ACTOR'S HOTEL ROOM. THE FOLLOWING MORNING.

I've just scrolled through what I wrote before last night's performance and I'm aware that my tone of 'hmm, not-quite-sureness' about the general state of things might make me come across as something of a grumble-buttocks. It's true there are many iniquities in the modern world which *literally* give me a stricture of the heart (soap stars are another. Dear God, you'd think they were Eleanora Duse to hear the way some of them go on about themselves. Smashing people no doubt, but given their often less than wonderful level of ability . . . I mean come on. True star quality is about rather more than making a pop record or getting some tabloid sports hack to write your autobiography for you – assuming the poor dolt can find anything at all to say about your meaningless little life..)

So, yes, there are bêtes noires in the Craig demonology, but I would be the very first to acknowledge that there have also been some enormous plusses in recent years; things that have made life that little bit more bearable for all of us, such as *Theatre de Complicite*, costume drama and on a more mundane level – cashback. We have also witnessed some tremendous advances in wine-cooling technology (those silver sleeves can chill a bot of 'poo quicker than Jonathan Pryce can do a *Daewoo* commercial) and finally, *finally*, Waitrose has agreed to stock organic pak choi – proof that well organised direct action *can* produce results.

Indeed, I have to say that since I last sat down to write about the unique role of the actor in society, the range of supermarket food products has improved out of all recognition. God alone knows how one managed in the past. The other day I clashed trolleys with Alan Rickman in Selfridges Food Hall and he reminded me that it's not so very long ago that you could walk the entire length of the Chiswick High Road without seeing a solitary piece of lemon grass on sale. If you tell that to young actors they look at you aghast. In fact I was doing a voice over with Alistair McGowan the other day and as he was swigging at a bottle of Evian water in between takes I pointed out that back in the dark ages when I first started doing ads for instant high-interest cash loans we had to do without 'Evi'. 'But what on earth did you carry in your hand when you walked into the studio?' asked an incredulous Alistair. 'Polos and a crossword' I replied. I think he thought I was mad. Of course, like Alistair, I'm a total Evi addict now and, indeed, I'm so neurotic about running out I invariably slip a couple of spare bottlets into my rucksack even if I'm only nipping down the road for a peep at a new gallery. I may take absurd risks as an actor but in many other respects I'm a right bleeding Carlotta Cautious Clogs.

So improvements there have most emphatically been in the contents of the actor's fridge – always assuming you have actually managed to scrape together enough money to buy any food or drink, that is. Because of all the advances that have taken place in recent years, they certainly have not been in the realm of fees. Try getting a reasonable rate out of Radio 4 for a day's work and you're made to feel as though you're asking for the Turin bloody Shroud. The merest demur and Sanjay and his chums from Artists Contracts start whining 'No way can we go to three hundred, my friend – Ian Holm's only getting three-ten.' And so on, and so on … I mean it really is unbefuckinglievable now. Good job I enjoy what I do, isn't it?

SCENE. INTERIOR DRESSING ROOM OF ACTOR TRYING TO BE POSITIVE IN THE LIGHT OF THE FACT THAT THERE IS NO HOT WATER IN THE SHOWER AND IN ORDER TO REMOVE MY MAKE-UP LAST NIGHT I HAD TO CRACK OPEN THE LITTLE ORMOLU FACE-WIPE DISPENSER THAT I BOUGHT AT THE GIELGUD AUCTION.

These are the circumstances under which I am expected to analyse the changing trends in acting over the past thirteen years while at the same time carrying out the intricate make-up and hair preparations for my own performance. The joys of touring! I suppose we oughtn't to grumble because great strides have been made lately in the science of make-up. The price of nose putty has come right down since the Koreans entered the market, and Kenneth Branagh has at last found a non-running liner which hides the fact that he has no lips. So there is much to be grateful for.

But to return to the main thread – the spinal cord – of my ruminations. The question begging to be answered is how has my approach to my work changed?

When the theatre reviewer from *Men's Health* magazine dubbed me 'The Blowtorch of the Barbican' I thought it was a bit OTT but now I'm not so sure. The fact is that in spite of all efforts to the contrary I can't help but scorch in performance. I could no more give up coruscating than I could curl up on the sofa and relax with a good book. No doubt it's a terrible failing but there we are. Despite sticking a note on my dressing room mirror at Mold last July saying 'Incandesce Less' I still ended up giving it the bloody lot in *Mrs Frobisher's Boudoir*. So much so that we had to issue a warning before curtain up and even then sections of the audience left at the interval. So I'm very conscious of the power I have as an actor to move large numbers of people.

I remain as rabidly and intoxicatingly left-wing as I was thirteen years ago – probably more so – and I'm still passionately committed to vigorous new writing (especially if it's Scottish) but my fervour tends to be laced with a little more pragmatism these days. So I'm afraid if they want me to take part in one of these fashionable capers that rejoice in the name of 'short films' I dinna budge from Richmond until a nice motor bicyclist has delivered a jiffy-bag plump with smackeroonies to number 12 Marchmont Road. The sad fact is that, as an actor, one has to protect oneself most carefully these days, and now that I've doddered into 'a certain playing age', I grab any opportunity I can to nestle away another little pot of crinkle-bunce for the Craig retirement fund. Things being what they are, I'd be bloody crackers not to.

Apart from that, I'm still pretty much the same foul-mouthed, brawling troubadour of old. Whether it's wading through a sea of syringes and crème fraiche as I did in *Fist F***ing* at the Royal Court in '94 or hosting an operetta cruise down the Danube as I did for Saga Holidays last spring, I still have a burning need to perform, to communicate and to immerse myself in all the roiling, squalid splendour of life – quite literally in the case of the notorious kitchenette scene from *Fist F***ing*.

My work has certainly responded to the changes in the last thirteen years and I suppose the next question begging for an answer is to what extent has my approach to my work changed the world?

I do not claim that it was our production of the banned dissident play *Six Days in Sçzsiòybîschèwscïe* in 1989 alone which brought an end to centuries of communist oppression throughout Eastern Europe but it probably marked the turning point more than any other single event. It somehow crystallized the moment when half a billion subjugated people from the Black Sea to the Baltic suddenly woke up and said 'No, actually. Sorry, but no. Wall down now please, iron curtain up THIS INSTANT!' It was humbling to be involved in such a planet-altering piece of rasping theatre. It was also a smashing company, and some of the first night presents we gave each other are among the most hilariously naff I've seen in twenty-five years of political theatre.

So *mutatis mutandis*, the old world keeps on turning, *tempus* continues to *fugit*, yet the shattering power of the actor in performance remains undiminished. The raw, rhesus positive lifeblood of ideas still thump-pumps through that invisible umbilical cord which connects the artiste to his audience. The history of the last thirteen years has once again proved that there is simply no one, be he politician, prelate or philosopher, who can match a classically trained actor as a force for radical change – providing he's properly looked after of course, which doesn't happen very often these days, if at all. Steven Berkoff told me that when he did *Dexter and the Aliens*, the day bed in his Winnebago must have been designed by Torquemada, such havoc did it play with his coccyx. You see, the real architects of revolution are never truly appreciated.

There are those who mellow as they get older (Zoë Wanamaker would be a good example of that) but I'm afraid N. Craig appears to be getting even more reckless and indiscreet. The fact is I'm 49 and I don't give a figging toss. I play what parts I want, how I want with as much facial hair as I want, and if you don't like it, matey, you needn't buy a ticket. I just love it that no bugger knows quite which way I'm going to jump. People expect to see me giving it the full-on lungs and leather treatment on a main-house stage, but I'm equally excited by the raw electricity of small-space work. On the one hand I relish doing the kind of thought-provoking play that challenges the audience's preconceptions about art and the nature of friendship – alternatively I'll just as happily say 'bollocks to that' and go and do twelve weeks in *ART*.

Each and every one of my friends told me it was madness to go into *ART* with Nick Bateman from *Big Brother* because, they said, he'd never acted before – well I'm here to tell you he learned damn fast, and we made a right rascally duo of Nicks

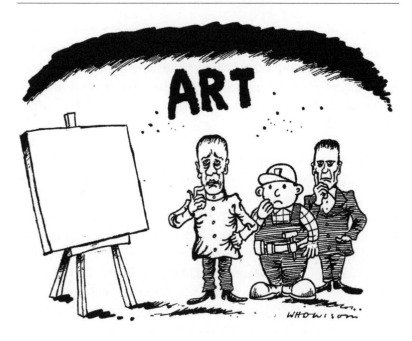

Nicholas Craig, Bob the Builder and Nasty Nick in Art.

('Nice Nick, Nasty Nick' as it said on the poster). We got on famously. The problems in the production – and they were by no means trivial – were caused by the sudden unavailability of my old mate Nicholas Le Prevost (Not Quite so Well-Known Nick, as it was to have said) and management's inspired decision to cast a life-sized model of Bob The Builder™ in the key role of Ivan. Despite one's very best efforts it has to be said that the occupant of the lovable handyman outfit and I did not get on. Lateness in the theatre is unforgivable. Sometimes Nick and I waited in all morning during rehearsals only for Friend Yellow-Hat™ to appear with the lame excuse that he'd developed a streptococcal infection. Well, if someone is really ill I'm as sympathetic as the next man but when I opened the *Standard* and saw a picture of Mr Builder™ opening a DIY store earlier in the day a certain curdling occurred in my personal tub of the milk of human kindness. Once we even had to delay the start of the actual performance by a quarter of an hour which had a disastrous knock-on effect as it just isn't possible to keep eight hundred city analysts and consultants in a theatre after half past nine at night, however inconsequential the plot and simple the arguments. I hope he trips and falls on his bloody cordless drill.

Despite dire predictions and isolated acts of vandalism from certain dungareed construction workers, the theatre thrives. Perhaps the most exciting recent development is the stunning nudity that the Americans have brought to the London stage. Nicole Kidman, Kathleen Turner, Darryl Hannah, Amanda Donohoe and Jerry Hall have all jetted in and been superbly naked in both the West End and the fringe. Nicole Kidman stripped off for David Hare at the Donmar theatre for only two hundred pounds a week, which was fantastic and makes you wonder what lies in store for theatre-goers once Nicole's agent gets her act together. Pure theatrical viagra, the critics said, so it's hardly surprising that they want her back, and it could well happen. The theatre is extremely handy for the Piccadilly Line link to Heathrow and as soon as Concorde is back in service, Nicole will be able to walk out of her apartment in Manhattan and in less than five hours she could be flat on her back at the Donmar, in her birthday suit with Joe Fiennes on top of her. I mean the speed of it is just astounding. It would have taken Sir Donald Wolfit *weeks* to manage all that. Kathleen, Darryl, Amanda and Jerry have also kept their ends up at the Gielgud, dispensing not so much pure theatrical viagra as pure theatrical evening primrose oil – less spectacularly effective than Nicole's dosage but much, much longer lasting.

People complain about Americans coming over here and taking the bread out of the mouths of naked British actresses ('underdressed, underpaid and under Joseph Fiennes' is the girls' tired old whinge), but I think we should be grateful so many Hollywood folk want to settle here. Just look what it's done for property prices. I had a valuation on Marchmont Road the other day and guess what the man from Foxton's said? One-point-one. ONE-POINT-ONE, I kid you not. Bought it for forty-five in 1982. So anyone who complains about being swamped by naked Americans obviously hasn't got a five-bedroomed house in Richmond to sell.

Whether they act with or without their clothes, there's no doubt that female actors generally get a better deal and are better served by writers than used to be the case. Any gender fortunate enough to have David Hare writing for it can't have too many complaints. Some of David's recent plays have not only presented the woman's point of view with penetrating clarity, they've even done so in the west end, albeit briefly. David writes with such uncanny understanding about women that one could almost believe he is one. He isn't a woman of course – that would be a ridiculous thing to suggest. They wouldn't let him into the Garrick Club if he were a woman and although he'd get into the Long Room at Lord's nowadays it's still absolutely idiotic to suggest that Sir David Hare is female. Let me be clear about this: **DAVID HARE IS NOT A WOMAN**. I'm not saying David's a 'regular guy' or a 'man's man' because I think that gives the impression of some sort of ghastly hairy-arsed Casanova, and he's far more spry and sensitive than that – Oh Lor! Now I've made him sound like a slightly camp vicar. It's so hard to pin David down in words but if you can imagine Sir John Galsworthy in Nicole Farhi briefs with no visible knicker-line – but then again, you see, even that doesn't begin to do him justice as a writer.

It is of course mainly due to David that fringe theatre is enjoying a golden age to match the 1590s but there are writers several generations younger than David bullocking their way through and winning the hearts of critics throughout North London. I recently went to the King's Head theatre to see the debut of one of the new bullocking Irish playwrights. *The Beer* used a deceptively simple device of two unremarkable old men at a bar talking about fags, football, sandwiches – and of course beer. Simple, as I say, but absolutely riveting. I sat spellbound until the landlord asked me if I wouldn't rather go and see the play going on in the back room. I was reluctant to exchange my comfy stool at the bar for a section of radiator at the back of the auditorium but I'm glad I did because, even though I had to pay fifteen quid plus a fiver to the appeal fund, and even though a woman next to me spilt Guinness down my neck and stubbed her roll-up out in my rucksack, *The Beer* proved to be a broth of a brew. The two men talking about fags and booze were perhaps not quite as well matched as the two I'd seen in the bar but their posture was in a different league altogether. The play instantly placed Connagh Comishen (its bullocking author) up there with the likes of Cyril Fletcher and Pam Ayres as a wry monologist. I had a quick pint with Con afterwards just to say well done, mate, have you written another one yet and if so what parts are there in it exactly? He hit me with his outrageously ambitious plan to introduce a third Irishman to the cast, and, if you please, to set the play in a completely different pub! Well, bugger me if he didn't go and do it. Not with me sadly, but I've kept in close touch because I understand Con's going to tackle a leaving do next. Watch this space, bigorrah!

I have a truckload of respect for playwrights. I don't think they always get the credit they deserve for the helpful contribution they can sometimes make to a play. Of course a lack of social skills and a limited wardrobe, plus the odd bit of food in the beard can make a playwright feel slightly awkward in large groups of people. I've noticed that when a gaggle of actors are really sparking each other off – telling anecdotes and singing songs from the shows in different regional accents – playwrights can simply get more and more tongue-tied. I can recall a striking instance of this a few years back at Ian McKellen's housewarming out at Wapping (sweet little place – such a shame he could never find a way of bringing it into town). We were all nattering away and I noticed the great American writer David Mamet looking increasingly ill at ease reading the video titles on the bookshelves. I went over to him and, just to relax him, asked what he was up to but he just spat in a plant pot and carried on whittling a hickory stick. Gradually I managed to get him to open up and realised he was a pussycat really; not much to say for himself but with a steady gaze and a profound affinity with the natural world around him. A bit intimidating you could say. But I persevered and a few days later I found myself going on an ice fishing trip with him. His only words to me all afternoon were 'big fish, bad fish' as he baited up a hook and tossed it through the drill-hole in the frozen Serpentine. What does one do in a situation like that? I hadn't used a meat hook since *Fist F***ing* but I must have *looked* as though I knew what I was about because, calooh callay, David cast me in his next play. Which I'm ashamed to say was the sole reason I spent so much time cultivating him (and it was bloody hard work paying poker all night then tramping miles through the woods in a checked shirt, I can assure you).

I can't remember what the play was about except that it had the chattering classes absolutely riven from stem to stem. There were fights on the steps of the Royal Court, people hurling glasses of Pays d'Oc and bruschettas at each other and the arguments filled the *Guardian* for months. I must say that's exactly the kind of theatre I like; inflammatory, issue-based, a hint of Mediterranean flavouring and no risk of being tied to a long run in the West End.

It was through David that I eventually received a call from Channel 4, which was to plonk me at the very epicentre of TV mover-and-shakerdom. Although the story has a happy ending it was emphatically not an experience I would care to repeat. It happened thus:

The car arrived at Marchmont Road one night just as *Newsnight* was finishing and half an hour later N. Craig found himself in a smoke-filled studio playing, of all things, celebrity poker in front of the cameras. They put me between David and another manly playwright from this side of the pond, Patrick Marber. Once again I made myself agreeable to Mr Marber because, not to put too fine a point on it, he was hotter than one of Simon Russell Beale's Mexican dips at the time and basically I was after nabbing him to write a sitcom for me. It was probably because he was racking his brains for an idea that the daft ha'p'orth failed to check his raise when Amanda Burton had her ace of spades on the table. I folded strategically and Patrick and I snuck off for a bottle of whisky in the green room.

We lit a couple of cigars and caught up on the goss. He was absurdly sweet about *Fist F***ing*, saying he thought the scene with the hedge trimmer and the squaddies was as fine as anything I'd ever done. I returned the compliment with some little dollops of jam about *Dealer's Choice* and with the merest nudge on the tiller I was able to steer the conversation onto the subject of sitcom. I took Patrick through the essential ingredients as they appeared in the BBC's demographic guidelines. My character, I felt, should be a middle-aged man who worked in the media and had a cynical take on the world that stemmed largely from a deep sense of self-loathing. The sympathy for the character would spring from the fact that he had plenty of money, dressed like a teenager and was incapable of lifting a finger for anyone else. I also thought it was vital that we steered well clear of hopelessly outdated 'funny lines' or, God help us, 'satire', and that we shouldn't be seen to be trying to get 'laughs' so much as scornful snorts of recognition. I also felt that the humour should come not from wearily contrived set-pieces but from realistic situations like when he ran his children over in his Saab, or when he played keep-up with a football during his mother's funeral service, elements that I felt gave the show a cool and unblinking nineties savvy.

Over a couple of days' whisky-fuelled mallard shooting on Hampstead Heath, we began to lick *A Very British Dude* (my title) into shape. They were heady times – hunting, drinking then diving into the Heath's famous bathing ponds to clear our

I sometimes think I would like nothing more than to rehearse every day for the rest of my life.

heads. I'd only ever swum in the Mixed Pond or the Men's Pond before but Patrick sneaked me into the Playwright's Pond which was enormously invigorating. The water had a slightly bitter taste and a miasma of pipe smoke hung above the surface, creating a peaceful if slightly melancholy atmosphere; the silence disturbed only by the echo of cricket commentary coming from radios around the banks, and the occasional desperate and frankly embarrassing incursion from the Actresses Pond.

I decided to pitch *British Dude* to my great mate and favourite lunch companion of all at the BBC, Sophie de Romanoff Khan. She, too, was hot as a newly toasted pikelet at the time in spite of – or perhaps because of – the fact that she had never actually made a programme. But she has a wonderfully sexy laugh and a castle in Ireland so she was always destined for higher things. She still hasn't made a programme, incidentally, and it's unlikely now that she ever will – her contact list is so vast and influential that if she committed herself to one particular project in favour of another it would spark off a chain reaction of jealousies that would just ruin her fabulous parties. But Soph has always been terrific at putting a bit of heat under things, and sure enough, four lunches at Bibendum later, she had assembled a team of executive producers, script advisors and bi-medial planners who all gave conditional assent to putting the project under review. Within six months the Beeb decided to green light a focus group report on the typeface for the title page of the script. It was very exciting. A year later, when we were literally a month away from setting up a lunch meeting to discuss which directors to take out to lunch, Patrick dropped a bombshell. We were sitting in wicker chairs on the pontoon in the middle of the Playwright's Pond, authors swimming silently around us with their beards glistening in the late afternoon sunshine. Patrick took a long sip of his whisky-sour and said he'd never really liked the idea of *A Very British Dude* and since he'd workshopped four plays and a film script in the meantime he was off to America to direct them. Which, I'm afraid shows just how much he still has to learn about television.

Devastated, I did a couple of desultory circuits of breast-stroke with Arnold Wesker – who'd also just had a rejection – then rolled up my bathers and towel and trudged forlornly off towards Hampstead Heath station to get my Silverlink back to Richmond.

Now I said the story had a happy ending and we are now closing on it at a rate of knots. As I was toddling down Fox Walk who should I bump into but my old mucker from *Fist F***ing* days, Harriet Rackstraw. We fell a-nattering and a-gossiping and before long we were hooting with laughter at the memory of the night Craig clean forgot to bring the bag of squirrels on and Hat, poor darling, had to improvise as best she could with a pillow-case and the squaddy's bayonet *and* she had to do her own squeaks. Into the midst of this unseemly display of anecdotal hilarity whizzed a bicycle bearing another esteemed mate from the past, the inimitable Bill Wackerbath (he was en route to Kenwood House where he has special permission to play the virginals). Before we knew it we were scheming like crazy and the upshot is that, without the aid of a single lunch, Hat, Bill and I are going to do an evening of theatrical anecdotes at the Festival Hall in December as a pre-Christmas treat. It'll be a veritable gallimaufry of thespian fun and frolics with sonnets, cat poems and the occasional surprise, plus a stocking-filler or two from Mr Wackerbath at the piano. Not a bloody soap actor in sight. What an unusual evening that's going to be.

SCENE: INFERIOR HOTEL ROOM. MORNING.
Just had a scrolleroony through the text so far and I feel I should leave no one in the slightest doubt that whatever the limitations of certain soap performers my belief in the medium of television is total and passionate. Indeed it's a source of immense personal pride that, within my lifetime, we, the working class, have taken control of TV and turned it into a populist expression of our shared experience, of the zeitgeist if you like, although I hate that word.

I revel in making the kind of shows that enrage the cultural mandarins but which the so-called great unwashed (us) happen to enjoy watching. Soaps, for example, say what you like about the leading actors (although I think it's now against the law to criticise them), soaps are enormously important. They are nothing less than the psycho-dynamic templates by which we cathartize our teleology and anyone who can't see that is just a bloody snob. I haven't the slightest doubt that if Euripides were alive today he'd be writing for *Emmerdale* – and what's more he'd be the first to suggest going for a giggly ruby after the recording. So if anyone asked me if I had any objections to appearing in a soap, even as a visiting character, I would say yes. Not 'yes' I have objections, but 'yes' I'd love to read a script if there is one.

I also have a programme idea called *ACTORS GETTING STUCK!!!* which would show actuality footage of performers like Liam Neeson, Ralph Fiennes, Russell Crowe, Michael Kitchen and Tim Piggott-Smith in life-threatening situations such as floods, mudslides and ordinary household accidents which can be very nasty indeed. And much as I'd like to see that happen I'd also love nothing more than to slip into an Inverness cape, head for the cultural high ground and do another smashing costume drama. For me, doing a TV costume drama is about as good as it can get beyond the confines of a theatre and it's probably true to say that some of the most fulfilling moments of my professional life have been spent in gaiters and a stovepipe hat.

Costume drama really has been the success story of the last decade and a bit and it's been my very great privilege to notch up a pretty full dance-card of appearances. I positively salivate at the prospect of working as part of a team to create that invigorating smack and tang of period authenticity. It's been well documented that I am a confirmed rehearsaholic and so the meticulous preparation for a grand ball scene, complete with authentic skipping dances, transports me to the very gates of paradise. When I played Ebenezer Tumblewhiskers in *Dashington Manor* it took weeks to learn how to co-ordinate the dance steps while dabbing my brow with a hanky and repeating 'A capital ball! A capital ball!' It was just so frustrating that I never quite managed to steer Ebenezer's dog-cart in the right place so that it convincingly overturned the big pile of cabbages in the market scene, but I think they had it covered with the escaping hens.

With any much-loved novel there are always likely to be complaints about the dramatisation. In our case, most of the grumbles were about the way we replaced so much of the original narrative with grand ball scenes. You can't please everyone, I suppose. And in fact the producers had so many problems with the casting we nearly didn't make the series at all.

The role of Mr Dashington absolutely cried out for one of the Fiennes brothers but Ralph and Joe were busy and so the casting department turned instead to another great acting brotherhood, the McGanns. Though every bit as talented as his elder siblings, Tristram McGann is very much the black sheep of the family as a result of having gone to Oxford and worked exclusively in children's music theatre. However, filming coincided with the school holidays and we were able to lure him into the breeches and frock coat. Tristram's Dashington was superb. When it comes to casting a meaningful glance across a crowded ballroom he leaves Colin Firth standing, and he's an absolute demon with a butterfly net in his hand. It was an extraordinary coincidence that when they came to cast the character of Silas Whelk (Mr Dashington's arch-enemy who deviously takes possession of Dashington Manor), the first, second, third, fourth and fifth choices for the part were the other McGann brothers but as they, too, were unavailable we ended up with the black sheep of the Fiennes family instead. It's no secret that Darren Fiennes has never really hit it off with his younger brothers and that he's never had much family support for his decidedly *risqué* nightclub act. Darren's not the easiest person to work with, the endless blue jokes can get a bit tiresome and he drove make-up mad because he wouldn't allow a pair of scissors within a yard of his bleached mullet – but talent by the tumbrel, no question.

The publicity shots for the series were some of the cleverest I've ever come across – the main cast including myself, Tristram McGann, Darren Fiennes, Sharon Cusack and Fatima Redgrave, all standing in the mud holding styrofoam cups and showing our filming boots under our costumes – just brilliant. I'm sure that photo will make the cover of the Radio Times when they eventually find a slot for *Dashington* – which can't be too far off as it's now nearly five years since we made it.

There is plenty of room for so-called high and low culture on telly. The medium is easily large enough to accommodate the *Dashingtons* and the documentaries as well as the soaps and the *ACTORS GETTING STUCKS!!!* So rather than bickering over whether Keats was a better pop singer than Bob Dylan we should celebrate our cultural *smörgåsbord*.

I would also like to congratulate the BBC on their bold initiative, currently advertised in cinemas and on the backs of Persil packets, to go round the country recruiting complete amateurs to be actors, writers and presenters. It'll bring a much-needed breath of non-elitist fresh air to the corporation as well as saving the taxpayer a fortune in fees, and after all how else are we going to unearth the new Robson Greens and Ross Kemps?

So I'm extremely optimistic about the future for the performing arts in general, and on a personal level so many exciting possibilities beckon I have to keep slapping myself to believe it's true. There is a chance of doing another play with Jeffrey Archer which I'm very excited about as I always find working with convicted criminals 'on the in' immensely inspiring. Jeffrey has quietly turned himself into one foxy little actor in recent years, and I fully anticipate sparks flying round the day-room at Belmarsh once we start rehearsing. So there's that, and I might do a series of TV railway journeys (*In the Tracks of Edwina Mountbatten* has been mooted). There's the cat poems evening to look forward to with Bill and Hat in December, my personal TV arts odyssey *Chopin and Fokine* is currently being repeated every hour between six a.m. and midday on The Performance Channel, all of which is, as they say, better than a poke in the eye – another memorably searing image from the second act of *Fist F***ing*, by the way.

The tour ends in a few weeks time, so I'll grab a quick blast of sun in Lesbos then after that, who knows? I'm always dying to dive off in all sorts of different directions. Another costume drama would be nice, a soap as I say, a medieval French musical or a lovely film. Anything. Perhaps not a tour though.

In the meantime I dedicate this new edition to the individual I still regard as the most influential on our planet; the person with the power to inspire great deeds, to topple dictatorships and crush a prejudice like a beetle beneath his shoe; I refer of course to the onliest vagabond barometer of the human condition – the actor.

NC. The Micron Theatre, Oswestry, June 2001.

Wunderbar! The author hosts a Saga Holidays operatta cruise down the Danube. Maytime 2000.

PS. It appears I spoke prematurely when I said that the Methuen people were more cooperative than the last lot. I knew it was too good to last. 'Our computer won't recognise *Actorite 2000*' comes the bleating message, as though it's *my* problem! Evidently they don't teach typing skills at Bedales these days. One is, of course, devastated if anyone has to delay their departure for a lengthy weekend break in order to do a few hours of dictation but the fact is that some of us don't get weekends off at all, let alone weekends with Daddy in New York. Some of us have to give eight performances a week of *Ooh La La! Mon Colonel* at Oswestry, then spend the whole of Sunday on a train to Crewe, then change for Kendal and do another eight *Colonels* there and so on ad-bloody-infinitum.

I've just thought of something else that hasn't changed in the last thirteen years: the fact that it's always the actors who have to suffer. Extraordinary isn't it? Ho-hum, twiddly-dee, we survive.

I, An Actor

I

Early Days

My first appearance was in the South London Hospital. I am told that I bawled lustily and instinctively from the diaphragm.

My first role was that of a cloud in a nursery school production, the title of which escapes me. Indeed I remember nothing of the experience, however, my mother tells me that I was an exceedingly effective cloud – at any rate until my little white breeches somehow came unbuttoned and I inadvertently 'revealed all' to the assemblage!

My upbringing was rather an unusual one. My mother was, and still is, a quite remarkable woman, and my father was an exceptional man in many ways. I myself was by no means an ordinary child. One way and another, we were a pretty oddball collection of people.

From the start, Mim (my mother) and I were very close. We shared the same jokes, the same interests, the same gardening gloves. My father was always rather a remote figure. I never quite saw eye to eye with him and I think he rather resented Mim and I being so inseparable and the fact that we used to tease him, not always kindly, in our own secret language. It was a great shock when, right in the midst of preparations for my fifth birthday fete, he upped and left us for good. It cast a slight pall over the festivities, but somehow we got through.

So, all of a sudden, Mim and I were left on our own with no one to look after us.

Fortunately, there was no shortage of relatives to rally round

NICHOLAS CRAIG
AS
LORD FOPPISHNESS

when we were in a fix, as we frequently were. Darling Mim, though possessed of the kindest nature imaginable, was always apt to go haring off on some madcap scheme which was *guaranteed* to solve our problems. Nothing, but nothing, would deter her from these mad rushes of enthusiasm. They became known in the family as 'Mim's Hairies'.

I remember one morning at breakfast – this would have been when I was about eleven – she announced out of the blue that the garage was to be tidied up. This, she said, would give us a bit more space and would generally be the making of us. Pleas about the mess and the work involved were swept aside, the garage was going to be tidied up and that was that. Except that it wasn't of course, Mim snagged her cardy on a nail and I nearly got a splinter. We got excessively dusty and the whole operation seemed to take hours.

A constant support during these happy but haphazard years was her eldest brother, Jack. He was an extraordinary man, who had worked for the Inland Revenue during the war and was a very keen blackberrier. Needless to say I was devoted to Uncle Blackberry, as he was always known. Then there was her second youngest brother, Uncle Pillowcase, another remarkable character, though somewhat impoverished, having at one point sunk everything he had into one of Mim's Hairies. And then there were my two boisterous but adorable cousins, Bread Sauce and Stanley Knife.

How I loved those summer outings to the Bagshot area! Uncle Blackberry at the wheel of his Godfather's Lanchester, Mim next to him and the rest of us squeezed noisily into the back; the leisurely picnics (luncheon meat and dripping sandwiches have never tasted as good somehow); the compulsory blackberrying expeditions, organized of course by Uncle Blackberry; and then perhaps on the way home we would stop off for tea at Auntie Thirteen-Amp Fuse's bungalow in Egham. Golden days!

Above: *Uncle Blackberry.*

Left: *Mim.*

Unwillingly to School

School was to me an infuriating interruption of my blissfully happy home life. I couldn't wait for the final bell to ring so that I could rush home to Mim and hear about her latest Hairy.

I remember being called into the headmaster's study once to account for my general recalcitrance. The Sausage, as we called him, said to me, 'You really are a very strange boy, Parsons. I wonder what you intend to do with your life.'

With all the confidence of youth, and not a little asperity, I replied, 'I want to leave this place with all its untalented people as soon as possible and become an actor.'

The author, aged six, at Woolacombe Bay.

Mim in her 'Dancing Years'.

He laughed. If you are reading this now, Sausage, I wonder if you are still laughing.

The only thing which made my schooldays bearable was the school play. I distinctly remember my first Nativity play in the juniors. My Shepherd was a great success – until my hessian tunic accidentally slipped and I inadvertently revealed, shall we say, rather more than the plot!

I had to wait until I was in the senior school for my first triumph. It was in a production of *The Browning Version*. The frock, the shoes and the cami-knickers were all provided courtesy of Mim, and I think my Mrs Crocker-Harris was as good as anything I had done to date. It was all a great success, apart from one moment of utter mortification when, being unused to the cami-knickers, I inadvertently afforded the audience a full view of my masculinity – at no extra cost!

It was probably because of this incident that The Sausage awarded the acting prize to another boy. I was bitterly disappointed, especially as the whole family was out front; Mim, Uncle Blackberry, Uncle Pillowcase, Bread Sauce,

Stanley Knife, Auntie Thirteen-Amp and someone I hadn't met before called Grandpa Trousers.

We are going to move on now to the analytical part of the book. The reason being that my publishers have charmingly told me that no one will be interested in my comprehensive family history charts, nor in my holidays in North Devon with Mr and Mrs Business-Panther and the afternoons spent in their rambling garden (so perfectly suited to the game of 'Donkey's Slippers'), nor in the puppet shows I used to perform in front of the family – all of which I have taken great trouble to chronicle. Well, I'm the last person to want to bore anybody, and since I'm only the author (a very minor cog in the publishing wheel, I'm discovering), into the bin it all goes and on I shall press. Satisfied, Lucinda?

Richard II *(Glasgow Citizens, 1980).*

2
Essential Acting

'And the winner is – if I can get this open – NICHOLAS CRAIG for *The Cuckolde of Leicester*.'

In the crowded ballroom of the Dorchester Hotel, his thoughts swimming in a sea of loveliness, stands Ego.

'Why me?' he says, 'pourquoi moi? I'm just an ordinary working actor. I don't deserve this.' It feels wrong somehow and, notwithstanding his tears, his yelps of joy and his desire to kiss everything in sight, Ego remains detached from the scene, aloof – like a kestrel who says, 'What's all the fuss about?' then flies on to the next cornfield.

Ego weaves his way towards the stage. As he does so, he catches sight of himself in one of the mirrors on the wall. Ego pauses. 'Aha!' he says, 'so that's what someone looks like when they are about to receive an award. Better store the image away in the mental filing-cabinet for future use.' Always the observer, you see, always the Actor, always the job must come first. Cynical perhaps, but it pays dividends in performance.

A patent leather stagger to the stairs. On the first a semi-stumble (Côtes du Rhône). The second – better now, calf muscles moving into rhythm.

Now Ego is on the stage and walking swirly-burly. A thought. What a strange word 'stage' is: sta-ge, sssssstttttt aaaaaaggggggeeeeeeee, stage.

Trembling, Ego reaches the microphone (so no need to

project). 'Must speak,' thinks Ego, 'must kiss. No, must speak first – then kiss.' Words tumble.

'Deeply honoured ... sweat and love ... wonderful stage management ... clever little chap who made my hump ... approval of one's peers ... smashing company ... wanton destruction of the planet ... and that horrid mini-roundabout they've put on top of Richmond Hill ... bless you.'

Kissing, clapping, hugging, patting. All for *I, an actor*.

As an actor, of course, every fibre of one's being is revolted by the very notion of awards. Art is not competitive. There should be no prizes. So, to see it engraved on a bronze statuette that one is a better actor than Jeremy Irons (it doesn't actually say that, but that, effectively, is what it means) is simply embarrassing for both of us. It's absurd. I've seen Jeremy be bloody good in some shows, I'm sure we all have.

Nevertheless, I have won the bloody thing, no point pretending I haven't. It hangs like a glittering millstone around my neck, and however much I abhor the idea of it, however much I try to conceal it with invitation cards and however much I hate this horrid expression 'major talent', there it is, indelibly engraved in letters of gold: BEST ACTOR IN A HITHERTO UNPERFORMED LATE-JACOBEAN TRAGEDY – 1986. NICHOLAS CRAIG.

For hundreds of years, scholars have striven to define what it is that sets actors above the common herd, why it is they need to 'act', why it is that we need them to 'act', whether they do, in fact, 'act' at all or whether they simply 'dress up and shout a lot'. And yet to my way of thinking, none of these learned gentlemen has come near to unravelling the mystery. It is for this reason that I have taken the bold – some would say treacherous – decision to rip the covers off the acting profession, to reveal the darkest secrets of 'The Craft' and to show our actors in all their raw, noble nakedness. Check your seat numbers, it's going to be a bumpy ride.

In addition to Olympic fitness, supreme courage, phenomenal powers of concentration, the acceleration of a puma and an insatiable appetite for sheer bloody sweat and grind and plain old-fashioned sheer bloody hard work, the actor also needs a supernatural ability to transform himself into another person; to 'other be'. Not simply to 'pretend' to be someone else but actually to 'enter' that person.

My great mate Bill Wackerbath, a smashing actor, tells a lovely story against himself which, to me, captures the essence of acting, of 'other being'.

Bill and Harriet Rackstraw had taken a punt out one afternoon on the river at Stratford. A boat full of noisy schoolkids passed close by, disturbing the peace. Bill, being Bill, playfully prodded their boat with his punting pole calling out (I wish I could somehow convey Bill's wonderfully idiosyncratic vowels – Pudsey with a hint of Webber Douglas but since I can't you'll just have to imagine them), 'Ye play cup-ball with your lives, ye rascals, for I am Duke Aldonzo' (a very clever quote).

Horror of horrors, the boat overturned and all the children, none of whom had a life-jacket on, were thrown into the water. In an instant, Bill had his top off and was leaping to the stern of the punt ready to dive in and save as many young lives as he could.

'No, Bill, don't!' begged a distraught Harriet, 'you can't swim.'

'I know I can't,' replied Bill, 'but I *feel* as though I *can*.'

Now the point of this story is that it shows the extent to which actors are able to 'other be' even when they are not actually on stage. Of course Bill very soon saw the wisdom of Harriet's adjuration and smiled at himself for momentarily having 'other been' the sort of heroic figure who jumps into the water to save drowning infants, which is of course no part of the actor's job. You see, in spite of (or perhaps because of) the fact that there was no matinee that afternoon, Bill had to give a performance, had to 'act', to 'other be'. And he read a super piece of Strindberg at the children's funeral.

The Theatre

Billions of years ago, when man made his first faltering efforts to haul himself out of the primordial soup, there was precious little in the way of subsidized theatre. Nevertheless, pre-historical carbon dating has revealed that very early on, while some men displayed a talent for hunting, others for building, cooking etc., one particular group was motivated purely and simply by an overwhelming desire to 'do it'.

Little has changed since then. While some youngsters spend their spare time running, jumping or reading, the budding thespian will sit for hours alone in his bedroom nursing his 'urge' to join a profession that will free up most of his morning so he can wander round Covent Garden trying on shoulder bags. Some of us – Geoffrey Palmer is one, I am another – wanted to 'do it' just as much at seven as we do now, but it doesn't get hold of most people until adolescence.

It is at drama school where one learns that the proper place for it is in the theatre; the actor's spiritual home, his Kingdom of Other Being; the stage door with its fluttering notice boards, the corridors heavy with the aroma of sweat and greasepaint, the auditorium with its yielding velvet smoothed by a million bottoms, its gilt cherubs, its firm pillars soaring up into the roof. Our backstage realm with its dark and secret places, the dressing rooms with their rough breeze-block walls, mirrors, scorching naked light bulbs, squeaky vinyl floors, jingle-jangle coat-hangers, the dark passages leading to the prompt corner (the *strict* corner with which there can be no arguing), the taut ropes stretching up into the flies, the trestle prop-tables groaning with swords, buckles, leather, cane skips bulging with breast-plates, thongs and those spiky balls on chains. This is our domain, our secret temple of adventure, our cathedral of nakedness, our special little place. *This* is where we 'do it'.

The Performer

You know it always slightly amazes me when I hear actors being referred to as empty-headed hysterics. I don't know how this myth got about, but it is certainly not borne out by my own experience. I have always found actors to be very serious people, withdrawn and shy. Of course, we are all desperately insecure and so a certain amount of camping about does go on by way of compensation but we are basically an immensely contemplative species. Our job (because it *is* a job, and a bloody hard one at that) is such that we must spend hours slyly observing raw life so that we can reproduce it on the stage in such a way that each and every member of the audience will say, 'Ouch! That's the Truth. That's hit me between the eyes. That's what I came to the theatre for – an experience both raw and purgative, like being put through a philosophical mangle, cathartic, exciting, primitive, ennobling. I shall certainly buy a ticket for the next play at this theatre and I shall be more than satisfied if it is only *half* as good as this.' Hopefully, they will also say something nice about one's own performance, but if they don't enjoy it and they don't return we have failed. To an actor, a seat without a bum on it is a bereavement of a kind. We even die a little ourselves and we mourn as only actors can. But of course we are all immensely resilient and so we soon forget about it. The important thing is just to get on with the next scene, play, series, industrial training film, crime re-enactment, whatever. It doesn't matter as long as we can just get up and get out there and just bloody well go and 'do it'.

Craig: Why do you act?
Ego: Who, me? Christ, what a question.
Craig: No, come on.
Ego: Um, well, to tell the Truth, I suppose.
Craig: How do I know that's not a lie?
Ego: Stop tormenting me. I don't know. I am an actor.
Craig: *Oh bah didon! Vous êtes fou, Copain.*

The Truth – I

The actor must know what it's *like* to be everything from a Mongol Emperor to an Elderly Passer-By, he must *know* how the Frenchman feels when the alarm clock goes off, he must know how the *alarm clock* feels, he must *experience* the pain of the carrot on the chopping board, or how is he to tell the Truth? The Truth is *the* most important thing. It is to the actor what paint is to the artist, what ink is to the writer, what cement is to the bricky. It really is very, very *important*.

It is not simply a question (as some people blithely imagine) of learning one's lines and saying them. The actor must *find* the *Truth*, seek it, scent it like a foxhound and pursue it mile after lung-bursting mile until he has it cornered, vanquished, at his mercy. Take a line like this one:

> '*My dear Algy I thought you were down in Shropshire.*
> *How ripping to find that you're up instead.*'

What is it like to have a friend called Algy? Ask around. Better still, look through the phone book and find someone called Algy. Get to know him. *Befriend* him. Go to Shropshire. Find out why it is so ripping not to be there. *Live the line.* The audience haven't paid to see people walking about in nice costumes saying amusing things, they want 'other being', they want rawness, they want THE TRUTH.

Now let us take another line which we all know and which we often rather glibly accept at face value:

> '*An' thus with gory blade slew I fell 'Hammet in 's*
> *pavilion.*'
>
> (The Cuckolde of Leicester, *Act 6, sc. 4, l 220*)

A little careful scrutiny will show that it is by no means easy to extract the Truth from this line because, not only is the speaker disguised as his twin brother (although which particular twin brother we do not know at this stage), but he is also giving a false account of what happened at Aleppo. So the truth in this instance is a veritable 'jewel in a ten-times-barr'd-up-chest'. The actor must compensate for the deceitful nature of the line by being even more truthful than he would normally be. A good actor will find this very difficult, since he is always immensely truthful in the first place. Therefore he has to go into a kind of overdrive – we call this 'Truth-pumping' and it is very dangerous if attempted by inexperienced actors, as I shall discuss later.

It will be seen then that the actor is constantly searching, questing, striving, like a workaholic Trojan beaver to uncover and present the Truth in all its grubby, blood-stained, awesome potency.

The Truth – II

Which is why I am always faintly flabbergasted when I hear (as I have done) this bizarre theory that actors are sometimes less than straight-forward, that they 'say one thing and mean another', that they are given to insincerity. Out of the very deep respect and love I have for you, gentle reader, I would ask you to be wary of this canard. Actors are in fact the most honest group in society. It is absurd to say that people like Roger Rees and Chris Barrie and Patricia Hodge are shammers. Look at Ewan McGregor, Martin Jarvis and Henry Goodman – humbugs? I think not.

Some people seem to think that because we are demonstrative and 'up-front' we are not genuine. Make no mistake, we are in deadly earnest. If we kiss each other it is because we love each other. A lot. It's as simple as that.

It's people *outside* the profession who are seemingly incapable of telling the truth. Publishers for example, who assure one that one's book is going to be printed on recycled paper and that the launch is going to be somewhere nice like

Coriolanus *('Understanding Shakespeare', BBC Schools TV, 1975).*

L'Escargot (where you get those little choccy snails afterwards) and then one finds out through rumour and third-hand gossip that this is not going to be the case at all, that there are going to be thirty fewer photos and that the launch is in fact going to be at some wine bar in Holborn *in the evening* when most people have to go to the theatre to perform. It just seems so silly when politeness costs nothing. One is on the phone, one is always willing to talk things over. I'm thinking of retitling this book *I, Someone Who Is Kept Completely In The Dark* because, surprise, surprise, yet again the actors are the last to know. Quite frankly I don't give a bugger about the chocolate snails but what does faintly enrage me is this widespread belief that actors are hysterical idiots who mustn't be told anything. Well I would like to go on record here and now as saying on behalf of my profession, and I'll put it in capitals because I think it's important: EXCUSE ME. WE *DO* HAVE BRAINS. WE ARE *NOT* ROBOTS, WE ARE *PEOPLE*. WE HAVE FEELINGS. IF YOU PRICK US DO WE NOT BLEED? IF YOU KICK US AND RUB DIRT IN OUR FACES WE FEEL THE HURT JUST AS MUCH AS ANYONE ELSE, PROBABLY MORE SO. I'M SORRY TO GET CROSS BUT IT'S JUST SO *UNFAIR*.

There. All over now, end of whinge, on with the book.

The Text

If we imagine the text as a huge chimney stack somewhere in the north of England, and the actor as a nude steeple-jack, his character as the dynamite which blows the whole thing up, his preparation in rehearsals as a huge trampoline, which stops him from hurting himself when the chimney comes crashing down, and the audience as a hungry lion with toothache pacing about underneath the trampoline – then we begin to get a picture of what an extraordinarily crucial animal the text is.

I cannot emphasize enough the concentration and sheer

bloody sweat and graft that needs to go into studying the text. We cannot go back to it often enough. Eat it, sleep it, love it, take it to the Caprice for supper, and, who knows, something rather lovely might happen.

The text. *The text.* THE TEXT. *THE TEXT!!!*

The Text as Script

There is nothing quite like lying in bed on a crisp autumn morning and being coaxed into wakefulness by the sound of a clean new script coming through the letterbox floppity-plop. It is like being a snow-tigress at the moment of conception; receiving the seed which joins with one's own and steadily grows within one for months and months, burgeoning, demanding, burdensome, fearful, until one day it bursts forth into the world in all its naked, animal, vulnerable beauty. I love scripts.

Some actors seem to have that 'oh-well-we-might-as-well-rehearse-it-for-a-bit-and-then-do-it-in-front-of-an-audience' attitude, which is so silly because they are cheating themselves *and* their audience by neglecting to carry out the vital, rich and rewarding work of studying and analysing the text. If any of those actors should happen to be reading this, I appeal to you – Tony, Ian, Jeremy, Mike – the text. The text. The text!

I have always been meticulous about reading scripts and, usually, I will read the other parts as well as my own – and sometimes whole scenes in which I do not even appear. I believe this is the only way to absorb a play. Make no mistake, there is no Royal Road to understanding a text, it is simply a question of graft and slog and toil and plain old-fashioned sweat, I'm afraid. Sorry, but there we are.

So much for new work. When one is going to do a classic text one will usually slip along to the bookshop (Richmond Pages is my local) and buy it. I make it sound a rather simple process but it is invariably one of the most traumatic experiences of

Gareth in his happy HUNTing ground.

Kernan the barbarian!

McKellen – nothing like a Dane.

one's entire life. I remember when I knew I was going to play Lord Foppishness I stood outside the shop for about six hours desperately trying to pluck up enough courage to go in and ask for a copy of *School For Fops*. Even though I was wearing sunglasses and a large fedora, I just knew they would recognize me and say something like 'Oh, so you're going to have a crack at Foppishness, are you? You cheeky bugger. You'll probably be quite awful and get deservedly poor reviews. Who do you think you are?' Finally, summoning up every last atom of raw courage I could muster, I got down on all fours, crawled into the shop and hid behind a huge pile of remaindered copies of *Tim Piggot-Smith's India*.

Then the worst happened. The girl had obviously recognized me.

'Can I help you, Sir?' she said, knowing perfectly well why I was there.

'Er, no thanks. Just looking at the plays, not that I'm going to be in any of them or anything, just interested.' I was in the most awful funk, knowing that everyone in the shop was looking at me and I scuttled behind the Christmas cards, turning my collar up.

Eventually the proprietor sidled over, clearly hell-bent on bombarding me with questions about *which* play and *what* director and *where* and could he have a photograph to stick up in the shop. Sweet, but yawn, boring, please God can you send a bus to come and run him over.

'Is there anything you seriously want to buy, Sir?' he said, by way of a preamble. That was it. My nerve snapped.

'Look,' I said, 'I don't know whether I'm ready for Foppishness yet, but at least give me the chance to try it. I deserve that at least. Come and see it, and if you don't like it, tell me and we'll talk about it over a drink, but please, please, my confidence is very low at this stage. Don't prejudge me.' With that, I flourished my cane at him and *literally* ran out of the shop. As my feet hit the pavement I realized that, without even having read the script, I had started to become Lord Foppishness.

The Chinese Meal

If actors are a noble priestly caste of fakir magician poets with the theatre as their temple and the stage their altar, the Chinese restaurant is where they have their dinner after the show.

The Chinese Meal is essential to the nourishment of 'Actor-

Family-Oneness' and is actually rather a complicated ritual. To start with, there will always be one or two people in any theatre company who, between you and me, are irretrievably naff and boring. It is obviously important that these 'Nafferoonies' remain unaware of any plans to 'go chinky after the perf'. They wouldn't enjoy it and so it is kinder not to ask them. It may be necessary for everyone to say false goodnights to each other and to leave the stage door in different directions.

There is a special skill in timing your arrival at the Chinese restaurant: too early and you have a long hungry wait; too late and you could find yourself stuck right on the end of a table with someone from wardrobe. The right time to arrive is when the first table has filled up and another one is being dragged across to make an extension. Plonk yourself down at the point of the join – you are then bang in the middle of the group, handily placed to leave or join conversations and to help yourself to a wide range of other people's food.

Always, always, *always* suggest that everyone digs into everyone else's and argue hard for the bill to be equally split at the end. It ought to be perfectly possible to consume £20 worth of food and drink while still only paying £10.37* like everyone else.

Actors' conversation, being unfettered and life-affirming, will usually cause other diners to fall silent, ashamed of their bourgeois values and enchanted by the exuberance of the 'theatre folk'. A kindly act is to draw them into your group by

---

*Of course these prices are a bit out of date but the principals of post-perf chinky etiquette are as infrangible now as when they were first codified – and as they will be for actors a thousand years hence. Although, in fact, I tend to eat far less Chinese food than in the past – they say they don't put MSG into things but they do and then of course you wake up totally dehydrated and spend the rest of the night gulping down gallons of Evian. Lebanese would be my post-perf cuisine of choice, or Moroccan, but I always insist on an assurance from the kitchen that the rice will be gluten-free and that they must never, EVER, mix cumin with harissa or use modified starch in the stock. I find that a lengthy discussion about my diet is a wonderful way to get the conversation off to a flying start.

waving or going over to their tables, kneeling down before them and begging for forgiveness in extravagant language. Try to sing the theme tunes from obscure Seventies TV shows, quote from other plays, and – of course – lots and lots of regional accents and silly voices.

Utter horror and complete embarrassment. I have been invited – Hat has not!

3

'The Nash'

Workshops to
rehearsals:

a liminoid world

Between Theater and Anthropology by Richard Schechner (University of
Pennsylvania Press, Philadelphia, 1985).

With my anarchic temperament, I had always thought that the
last thing I would end up doing was playing major roles at the
RSC and the Nash. Awkward customers such as me tend not to
have the happiest relationships with big institutions. Besides,
I have always preferred to remain a maverick, living from hand
to mouth, strolling from town to town like a troubadour of old,
singing for my supper, sleeping one night in a bejewelled four-
poster and the next in a hedgerow. I believe that living on the
razor's edge is immensely important for an actor. It keeps his
perceptions honed and his tool sleek. Just as, in days gone by,
mummers on the village green courted the wrath of the brutal
liege Lords, so should every modern performance carry a
similarly high risk factor. Put simply, a good actor must
constantly run the risk of being beheaded.

But after I had bought the house at Richmond I was faced

with such a massive decorating problem that working out of London was unthinkable. So when Sir Peter Hall rang in '84 and asked me to go to the National I was immensely pleased. Apart from the enormous prestige, it was only twelve and a half minutes away by chuff-chuff to Waterloo. And, Jesus F. Christ, the parts he was offering me! Lorenzo in *The Duke of Pisa* and Moonboot in Tom's latest, then Mr Atkinson in Alan's new caper, Towzha in the Cottesloe and finishing up with Lord Foppishness in the Lyttelton in November!!

'Sounds interesting, Peter,' I said, desperately trying to conceal my immense delight, for there is a Zen saying which has become my guiding principal over the last few years: 'Let the bean grow.' In other words, play it cool, don't rush into things. Besides, I never commit to anything without first getting drunk and phoning up all my friends in the middle of the night to get their views.

Most people seemed to think that if it was going to be in *The Duke of Pisa* it was sheer lunacy for me to play Lorenzo when the part of the Duke might have been written for me. Others thought I should play Antonio, while Simon was adamant in the view that I was a perfect Count.

In the meantime I, myself, had developed serious doubts about the Foppishness/Towzha double. So already weeds had appeared in the garden threatening to choke my bean. I had also decided that, in such a tiring season of plays (no sane person would undertake such a workload, surely), it was essential to insist on certain conditions: the use of the number one dressing-room throughout, an ionizer, an exercise bicycle, some decent curtains and (absolutely vital for maintaining performance fitness) lots of little presents and nice surprises.

I put all these points to Miriam, my agent, who said she thought we could also sting Peter for an osteopathic chair, a cassette/radio and a prawn and avocado sandwich for the interval of the Wednesday matinee. My experience has taught me to be cynical about such promises, but Miriam seemed

My agent, Miriam. 'A very tough cookie indeed.'

bullish, as she always does, bless her. She is a seasoned campaigner and one of the most feared negotiators in town. She started life in the Tennent's office just after the war and she has inherited much of Binkie Beaumont's cruelty, greed and charm. She also bears an uncanny physical resemblance to the great impresario and sometimes, when one walks into her office to find her wearing one of Binkie's suits and singing 'Pedro the Fisherman', the sense of *déjà vu* is almost eerie. But in a world of tinsel, of triumphs and of tantrums, it is her honest to goodness callousness that has kept her at the top of her profession.

The period when one's agent is haggling over terms is a very, very worrying one. One needs to draw on every ounce of raw courage one possesses – it's rather like being in the First World War. One lives with the constant fear that they'll make an offer to Charles Dance instead. But one has to fight these strategic battles in the overall campaign of one's career. I guess actors feel the same way about contractual disputes as the Tommies felt about those terrible battles in Flanders – desperately depressed if one lost one but wonderful when one won one.

'Peter won't budge on the ionizer,' said Miriam, 'and he says it has to be Lorenzo, but he's prepared to guarantee a vanitory unit in the dressing-room and he's offered a cheese bap in between shows on Saturdays.' This seemed to me to be so unbelievably small-minded I just flipped, and I'm afraid I shouted at poor Miriam for about four hours. 'Who do they think they are? Who do they think I am? I've been in this business for seventeen years and when I finish a matinee I'm *hungry*. Who wants to work at the National Bloody Theatre, anyway? National Car Park, more like. I've had more spiritual sustenance from a petrol station. You can tell Peter to stick his cheese bap right up his proscenium arch!' But Miriam had already put the phone down. I was so furious I had to do some K'Dang to calm myself down. Then, after about twenty minutes, I thought, 'Oh dear, I don't want to upset anybody. I'd better give in.' So I phoned Miriam and told her to accept. She said she had already done so, sly, wise creature that she is.

Four weeks later I started work on *The Duke of Pisa*, written in 1423 but very much a play for now, with Peter Hall directing.

One of Peter's greatest qualities as a director is the unobtrusive way he achieves his stunning theatrical effects. Throughout the rehearsals of *Pisa* he hardly seemed to say a word. This was because he was in Kentucky directing *The Barber of Seville*, but he still imposed his unmistakable stamp on our production in the way that the only greatest can. Before he left us he gave us his brilliant and deceptively simple view of the play.

'Listen boys and girls,' he said. 'We're only doing this load of old rubbish to get the critics off our backs for a bit, but we might as well make the best of it. As I see it, we can approach the play in three ways: a) set it in Nazi Germany; b) do it with red noses and white faces; or c) wear hand-made leather boots and cloaks and shout very loudly. Which is it to be?'

There was a general murmur favouring the leather and shouting approach.

'Done,' said Peter. Then he turned to the designer, said, 'three hundred thousand quid do you?' and with a wave and a puff on his cheroot he was away to the Blue Grass country.

We were left in the inexperienced but capable hands of Peter's assistant director, Simon Schawrtz. Simon was only just down from Oxford, but what he lacked in years he made up for in enthusiasm and intimate knowledge of Belgian court masques in the latter half of the sixteenth-century. His boundless energy was at once disarming and infectious. I think he would have rehearsed us twenty-four hours a day if he could. He was absolutely passionate about his work, and he once told me, half-jokingly, that he would poison his own mother if it would help his career.

Simon felt very strongly that we should make the production as 'Italian' as possible, so for seven weeks we worked on nothing but gestures and authentic Quattrocento whoops. The big Rialto scene was devastatingly effective, although it did feel at times as though we were just being stupid.

Peter returned the day before we opened and, though far too jet-lagged to see the play, he made some typically astute alterations. Personally, I felt he was wrong to cut the twelve hand-made Lambrettas, but getting nude boys to sell programmes on the Press Night was an inspired piece of showmanship which contributed enormously to the success of the play. The critics loved it.

'Electrifying!' was the verdict of the *Guardian* reviewer, to whom the occasion offered a long-awaited opportunity to list all the other fifteenth-century foreign plays he'd heard of. Simon's witty idea to have Antonio enter eating an ice-cream was dubbed a 'Coupe de Théâtre' by the *FT*. All in all, we were a hit.

Climbing the Mountain

For thousands of years actors have been preparing plays for performance by rehearsing. The ancient Greeks are known to have rehearsed. There is evidence that the Etruscans used to train for months with bronze weights attached to their arms in order to prepare themselves for rehearsals. In Tudor times the back room of a tavern was invariably where 'Will's latest' was licked into shape by the actors. The eighteenth-century actor Smythe wrote in his diary, 'I am determined to rehearse myself at Bristol, which resort hath a most easeful effect upon my quinsy.' 'Rehearsal breakfasts' were hugely popular with Victorian actors – lobsters, geese, potted mutton and potatoes were eagerly consumed before the day's work began. And yet so little is really known about the rehearsal process – those mysterious weeks in which actors and text fuse together to create a living, breathing performance or 'perforganism'.

Rehearsals are rather like being given a pair of skis and being told you've got to climb Everest then ski all the way down it again in two and a half hours without falling over or you'll be shot and eaten by jackals. In other words, they are as sickeningly frightening as they are physically punishing. Of course they can sometimes be enormous fun as well (I remember once on Harriet's birthday we had a cake and jelly and all wore paper hats to make it like a proper tea party), but for the most part it's just sheer bloody slog and blood and back-breaking, gruelling, numbing, plain old-fashioned bloody grind.

The rehearsal room is no place for the faint-hearted. You need strength to keep going when the coffee's running out and the workmen are drilling outside. You need stamina to carry on after lunch when the crossword's only a quarter done and you're ready to drop. You need self-belief, you need guts, you need animal determination and if you're playing the lead you need to make a cheesecake to show everyone that you're not starry or grand or anything, that you're just one of the cast, a worker.

Rehearsal Cheesecake

½lb crushed Edinburgh biscuits
1½ pints double cream
½ teaspoon vanilla essence
1½lb fromage frais de Toulon
Caramelized coriander
½ a maraschino cherry

3 goose eggs
½lb Spanish sugar
4¼lb butter
Fruit (try to find something
    that refers to the play)
Gelatine dissolved in Ouzo

Whizz it all up and pour it into a bain Marcel. Allow to set then decorate in a pattern appropriate to the play. Produce it at that time of the afternoon when everyone's a bit droopy and in urgent need of something nice.

Bill Wackerbath and Nicholas Craig demonstrate two basic crouches. Bill has adopted the RSC posture, while I (note the rolled up sleeve) am in the Nash posish.

The pressure on a principal actor to 'lead the ascent' is sometimes very great indeed. There is a very famous story about Albert Finney during rehearsals for *Genghis the Terrible*. For some reason, things were going slowly. Bacon's master-work had not yet 'caught fire'. Finney came in one morning dressed in full climbing gear; boots, crampons, salopettes, dayglo anorak, cagoule, ice-pick and seventy-five metres of nylon cord.

'Why are you dressed like that?' asked a puzzled Dennis Quilley.

'Because,' said Alby, chiselling a foothold in the wall, 'it looks as though I shall have to climb the f———g summit on my own.' There was general laughter but the point was well made and from that day on the cast appeared in rugby shorts and did forty-five minutes of abseiling down the side of the National Theatre's fly-tower before rehearsals each morning.

Rehearsal Diary: Base Camp to High Camp

There will be those who disapprove of the following section, those who think I am betraying trade secrets or in some way letting the side down. I regret any offence I may give but make no apology for telling the world at long last what rehearsals are really like – just what it is that actors get up to in Territorial Army and Sea Scout halls in the weeks before a premiere.

The Dogs of Tblonsk was a translation from the Czech of Hovel's satire on the conduct of the Tblonsk shipyard managers during the three-day strike of 1951. As with much iron-curtain drama, allegory played a vital part, all the protagonists being characterized, with deadly irony, as dogs. The play was something of a political time-bomb, so much so in fact, that every single Eastern Bloc theatre company had turned it down on the grounds that it was dreadful (Ministry of Culture-speak for dreadfully *true*).

The months leading up to the premiere of *Dogs* in the Cottlesloe were among the most rewarding I have spent in the theatre. It was by no means plain sailing, as the following diary extracts show, and I apologize in advance to those who may be offended by their content.

23rd October 1983

Having at long last finished reading *Dogs* I am in a quandary. Peter has offered me Towzha but without a doubt the part for me is Szpot. Trouble is, I think they've offered Szpot to Bob*. Oh God, what to do? I think the patio should look like this:

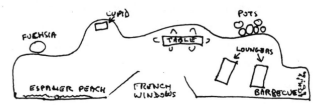

9.45 Bob rang in a state of high excitement re *Dogs*, saying he wanted Towzha. Since I am desperate for Szpot I suggested a swap. This could all work out very well.

24th October

A suspicion has been growing since last night that Bob is bluffing – only saying he wants Towzha to make me think it's a better part, and so have second thoughts about the swap. This would leave the way clear for him to play Szpot, which is what he has really been after all along, crafty bugger. If Towzha really is a better part, he surely would have pretended he wanted Szpot. I know I would have. Saw a bloody clever kitchen layout on TV this afternoon. It's sort of –

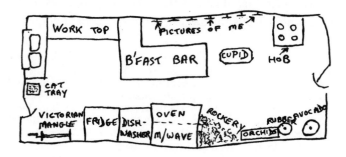

*Proudfoot

26th October

Rang Peter and said I'd rather do Szpot. He was silent for a moment and then said it was a pity because he was looking forward to my Towzha. Suddenly, I realized that deep down I wanted me to play Towzha too and that, as usual, I was just being silly, and I said as much to Peter. I apologized and will send him a bot of champoo with a little 'sorry' card and some flowers, a little piece of Staffordshire, a cheesecake and a pony for the children, and just pray that all is forgiven and forgotten.

27th October

I have just discovered that the director is to be Bill* with whom I cannot possibly work.

2nd November

Prelim meeting with Bill. I v. nervous but he v. courteous and full of nice remarks re me. We had rather a lot to drink and finished up having reconciliatory big huts, to the consternation of the waiters who must have thought we were made. I Love Bill.

4th January

Research begins in earnest today with a visit to Battersea with Bill and Bob. We are all very nervous, our minds blank canvases. The first shock comes when the supervisor of the dogs' home asks us, in the priceless way people outside the

---

*Bill Matlock directed *Irrelevance* at the Court in '78. We clashed over the interpretation of the scene where Marilyn Monroe explains the complex theory of bodyline bowling to an astonished Harold Larwood. Bill wanted me (as Larwood) to remain 'quietly proud', while I felt that the Notts express would have collapsed into a hysterical fit of remorse, torn at his clothes and rolled about the stage when confronted with his own lethal invention. Scripts were thrown, tempers were lost and Bill stormed off the show which was so silly but rather typical – such a shame because he does have talent and yet, time and time again, be blows it. But it was all right in the end because Christopher stepped in at the last minute and did a super production.

*Bill Matlock –
genius.*

profession have, 'What do you want?' I mean there we are on
Day One, absolutely no idea how we are going to approach the
text, only the vaguest thoughts on characterization. How can
we *possibly* know what we want? Inwardly Bob and I are
screaming at him; outwardly, of course, we are charm itself.
Walking along in front of the cages, we are all struck by the
extraordinary nobility of these animals. It is very moving. We
say nothing and Bob, who had a dog once, leaves our group to
be alone for a while. When he returns I make a little Hindu
'namaste' sign to show respect and greeting. In response, Bob
gets down on all fours and, growling, bites my trouser leg. Bill
laughs. I start to bark and howl which sets all the dogs off. It
is a shared moment. The supervisor comes running over.
'What the bloody hell's going on here?' he says.

'I'll tell you what's going on,' says Bill, looking hard at Bob
and I, 'we've just started work on *The Dogs of Tblonsk*.'

Bob and I stare at each other for a moment. 'By Christ, he's
right,' I say. 'There's no turning back now. This is the real
thing.'

The weeks that followed were a time of intense creative
activity with Bill, Bob and I meeting once or twice a week at
the kennels, the pub or anywhere in order to debate, argue and
prepare our equipment for the climb that lay ahead. Owing to

the absurdly short rehearsal time we had been given (fourteen weeks), we had to take many crunch decisions earlier than we would have wished. Gritting our teeth, we agreed that –

a) The first night party would be in the restaurant above the Cottesloe;
b) Everyone must have a proper long walk before each performance; and
c) We would award a silly prize to whoever was late for rehearsals most often.

23rd March

READ THROUGH!!!! I'm not superstitious about read-throughs but this does not prevent me from being reduced to a state of complete and utter quivering, jibbering terror. Most of the day is a blur of coffee and big hugs but a few random impressions remain: Harriet Rackstraw is in the cast, which is terrific news, Hat will make a brilliant Petra; rather a bossy designer measured us for our tracksuits and tails, didn't take to her greatly; Bill assures us (blessed relief) that we won't be on all fours; Bob makes a joke about rabies; a breathtaking reading from a young actor who is playing Szcep (Gary Something), obviously a talent to keep one's beady eye very carefully trained on.

6th April

Last two weeks have been hell – a complete waste of time for me. I am still floundering in the foothills. Cannot get the character. Towzha must be ambitious, lithe, ironic, analytical, noble, questing, earthbound, strong, a dog of ochre moods. I've tried playing him Pomeranian, I've tried Corgi, I even had a desperate stab at a Labrador which was an embarrassing catastrophe. And all the time Bob's Szpot goes from strength to strength. He is going to be entirely stunning. Never seen him so good.

I consult our technical adviser, Derek Hobson (who is also the co-creator and presenter of TV's *That's My Dog*). He listens calmly to my troubles, smiling and nodding occasionally. After about two hours of paternal indulgence, he puts his hand in his pocket, pulls out a photo and hands it to me saying, 'This is the largest of the Terrier group. Can you identify it?' Suddenly, like a bolt from the blue, the answer I'd been seeking for weeks comes to me. Road to Damascus – forget it. Burning bush – my bum. 'He's an *AIREDALE!!*'
'Correct.'

20th April

Sad news. We heard today that Simon Schawrtz's mother had died under mysterious circs. A smashing day otherwise.
Real progress. At last I have been able to respond to Bob's brilliance. Thanks to Derek Hobson my ascent proper has begun. I am starting to *live* Towzha, to feel him entering my bloodstream, to have his fears, his wants – I even had a good old roll in the garden this morning.
Disaster has struck, however. During an improv. session this morning I somehow got into a scrap with Bob and bit him severely.

27th April

Bill has used the whole of this week to work on barks and yelps. It's risky but I think it will pay off. Bill really is a remarkable man. One of the few directors who inspire an unquestioning loyalty among a cast. True, he is not the most fanatically hygienic *metteur en scène* who ever drew breath, but you somehow feel you would actually lay down your life for him if necessary, and tragically of course, four cast members of his mammoth *Culloden Trilogy* did so. He reminds me a lot of Rolf*; the same air of quiet authority, the

* Meyer. Skiing instructor at Col 1300.

same patient encouragement when one is trying to master a particularly tricky move. Bill's nod of approval at the end of a rehearsal session fills one with a very special pride. (I remember when Rolf presented me with my Wintasun medal at the end of the week, I felt so pleased with myself I thought I would burst, and it's the same with Bill.)

30th April
Went to see Bob in St Bartholomew's last night. He is recovering slowly and will be fit again for the first preview, though naturally very unprepared, poor chap. Awful to see him lying there, unable to move his arms and legs as, in a way, I feel sort of responsible. He said 'Nonsense' and we had big hugs, which hurt him a bit I think.
Everyone seems v. excited at the prospect of me being on *Wogan*. I, on the other hand, am distinctly under-whelmed. I am rather more concerned about the attitude of certain people on this production and the ever-increasing number of matters in which one's co-operation is simply taken for granted. That bossy cow of a designer –

The middle period of rehearsal is an enormously frustrating time, as any actor will tell you. You seriously doubt your ability to climb the mountain, still less your ability to make it down to the chalet and fondue without Rolf's reassuring presence.

It is an uneasy, worrying time. Differences of opinion do occur, tempers can sometimes be lost. Fortunately, one is professional and experienced enough to let these things just wash over one. My response to rows and flare-ups is simply to get my head down and press on with the Climb. Consequently my diary for most of May contains little more than trivial technical detail of no interest to the general reader.

29th May

Looks as though it's all blown over, thank God. The glaziers have been and gone, we've decided to use *paper* cups from now on, and everyone v. solicitous to me this morning. Bollinger from Bill, hug from Hat. A new designer has been engaged and I am to have the right kind of tail at last. Gary What's-his-name has been allowed to go, which I regret but he was unbalancing the production so much that we had no alternative. He will bounce back eventually.

1st June

Towzha comes on in leaps and bounds. Bill wanted me to enter normally but I think my instincts are right.

8th June

More bloody problems. The press office girls, in their infinite, have cocked up the *Wogan* interview. Not that I wanted for one minute to do the bloody programme – I hate it – but how on earth are people going to know the play's on if it isn't publicized properly? If truth be told, I'm deeply relieved but, really, one wonders where they get these girls from. I mean they sit in their comfortable offices surrounded by plants while the people doing the actual *work* are stuck out in some horrendous rehearsal room which is hopeless and miles from the tube. Actors are too bloody easy-going, that's the trouble. They just let themselves be pushed around and trodden on without a word of complaint. 'Oh yes, of course, Victoria. Anything you say, Caroline. How very stupid of me not to realize they might want to interview Charles Dance instead. Sorry for being such a nonentity. Shall I die here or would you rather I went round by the dustbins to do it?'

15th June

The new rehearsal room is a horrible airless dungeon

As Lord Foppishness in School for Fops *at the Lyttelton.*

underneath the Cottesloe. After lunch Harriet and I and some others started choking, staggering about, gasping and pretending to faint. I think we made our point. We are really up against the clock now. Only two weeks to the first preview. Bob has rejoined us from hospital and of course has masses still to do, poor thing.

The new Sczep is a boy with a rather strange face. He will be splendid.

22nd June
Summer has come at last – lovely morning (not that one sees any of it imprisoned down in the black hole of Calcutta).

Only a week to go. We are above the snow-line now but still very edgy about getting to the summit and back. Just as Rolf did, Bill has coached our push-offs and halts, nourished our faltering turns, pulled us out of the drifts, shown us the traditional way to drink Kummel, guided our forks to the little bits of sausage at the bottom of the pea soup. The question is, can we make ourselves worthy of the little Col 1300 Wintasun medals? Saw a bit of *Wogan!* Thanked God, Thespis and my trusty acting Geiger counter that I had the good sense not to appear.

Simon Schawrtz had some super news today. With the money his mother left him, he will be able to set up his own production company.

1st July
Second preview last night. I can see the summit only feet above me but I'm damned if I can reach it. Why? What is it that Towzha needs? A few more metres of rope? Some carabinos? An alpenstock? I don't know. Perhaps I'm afraid of reaching the summit. Perhaps it's Rolf's fault. Perhaps I'm snow-blind. Meanwhile Bob is putting together a really cracking Szpot. It is all very worrying. This should be a time of tingling excitement, a time of checking my rucksack for

the little Union Jack to plant on the summit but instead I'm standing helpless on the harsh barren slopes. The Alpine shrubs have shed their nourishing berries and I must dig out what roots I can for sustenance. Crueller hardships lie in store for us; food shortages and the unforgiving frosts will test our courage ere the sun returns and the first green buds appear on the rowan and Mother Earth bestirs herself for spring.

Audrey rang.

9th August

Even after six weeks of previews, tomorrow's first night fills me with unprecedented terror. I have taken a huge risk with Harriet's present, usually I give everyone little bits of porcelain but I saw a wonderfully hideous nodding dog in a petrol station which was so perfect I had to buy it. I just pray she likes it. Jesus, who'd be an actor?

11th August

Well, I got through it – but it was touch-and-bloody-go.

When Harriet opened my present I thought I detected a flicker of disappointment but her face soon broke into the broadest of smiles and she howled with delight. I got a 'doggie-do novelty' from her, and Bob gave me a little print of Lucrezia Borgia. I got thirty-four cards in all, Bill's was a priceless one of lassie saying 'Oh fuck, I've got the wrong briefcase!' Little Sue, the ASM, sent us all furry pigs and my dresser Winston gave me a pop-up Father Christmas which was rather rude' Ronco 'Buttoneer' and a Rex Harrison biog from Mim. Flowers from Peter and the men upstairs.

Usual first night panic as we struggled to get all the presents open in time for the performance. It wasn't until twenty minutes after the scheduled 'curtain up' time that we all scuttled down to the stage in our brown tracksuits and little black noses to give the first *Dogs* on British soil.

Hugs and hugs at the post-perf party. Someone said I

was the best actor this century, which was a bit of an exaggeration. Peter seemed overwhelmed. All he could do was pat me on the shoulder and say, 'Got a drink, have you?' before moving away, unable to express his feelings. Several other people seemed intimidated by the aura I was giving off. Oh my God, have I done it again?

The Holy of Holies.

4
Acto. Actas. Actat.

The stress experienced by an actor in the course of a first night is equivalent to being within one mile of a 2.83 megaton explosion – I can't remember the figures exactly but it is clear that during a premiere an actor is placed at enormous physical risk.

There are very few buildings which could withstand a nuclear strike of this magnitude. Why is it then that actors, stage-management and audience are able to survive such extremes of radiation and walk home from the theatre relatively unscathed? The answer is contained in one simple word – Professionalism.

Having said that, we are, after all, only flesh and blood and I think it would be wrong of me to pretend to you that I have always succeeded in living up to this great ideal of Professionalism. I admit that the last-minute tantrum has been a real friend to me on occasion, and any actor who has locked himself in his dressing-room and screamed, 'I am not going on until I get a wig that *fits*!' will be well aware of the enormous benefits which can accrue. No, I'm afraid that the leading man who eschews a modicum of last minute gamesmanship is a fool unto himself. What is the principal actor's function, after all, if not to create a little excitement? Keep 'em worried and they'll thank you for it, is my motto.

So what does it feel like to go through a first night?

As the curtain rises, a dark, mysterious hush falls and the

lights penetrate the black velvet abyss to warm the actor's face. It is conception, it is verse four of Genesis, it is an Atlantic breaker crashing over the sands, it is the breaching of the Moehne Dam, it is me.

The voice, initially perhaps a bit uncertain, the feet a little tentative, until the performance voltage starts to surge, the adrenalin to pump and the emotion to crackle and fizz and snarl and kick. Sometimes, as in Shakespeare (my first love), it's immediate and you soar over the many-headed like an electric monsoon. Sometimes it's more gradual – I remember when we did *Spring Affair* at Aylesbury, the sheet lightning didn't really strike until well after Reggie and Daphne had eloped.

Flying down the piste, concentration burning holes in the stage as you hurtle through the slalom poles. Please let me be good, please let me get it right, but always that nagging dread at the back of your mind that you have forgotten to give the stage management their 'good luck' cards. A gulp of Perrier in the wings – what a way to earn a living – and then on again, thrusting, burning, lunging.

Pushing up through Act Two now, exploring the recesses of the pauses, the sultry passages of the quiet bits. Oh God, I'm flying.

One scene to go. Quickly, slowly, *now*. AHHH. Done it. Time for half a fag and a hug in the wings, then back on for the curtain call. Run – stop – bow – hop. Again: run – stop – bow – hop. And again. Two more and that's it. Oh well, four more perhaps, now the panting, dripping smile that says 'Actavi. I have acted. Phew!'

First Night Presents: A 'What To Give Them' Guide

One of the abiding stumbling blocks of first nights is deciding what to give your fellow actors, some of whom you may not know terribly well. It is all too easy to drop a brick, as I did myself once when I gave Alan Rickman a vid of some ghastly costume melodrama – just for camp – only to find that Alan had quite a large part in the film. Result: egg positively oozing down the Craig phizzog. To spare others from this embarrassing fate, I have drawn on my own intimate knowledge of some of our leading players to compile this 'at a glance' guide:

Anthony Andrews: A lavishly illustrated history of our island race.

Alan Bates: 1930s luggage labels.

Kenneth Branagh: Money.

Eleanor Bron: Blackberries picked on a blustery, gustery day in September.

Simon Callow: plug spanners (unless it's the Scottish play, in which case chrysanths will do).

Julie Christie: Any of the works of R.S. Surtees.

Michael Crawford: Nice bath smellies.

Charles Dance: Has always wanted a mini-kettle for use in the dressing-room.

Edward Fox: Joss sticks.

Michael Gambon: Bits of old metal.

Sheila Gish: Absolutely anything by Tobias Smollett.

Jeremy Irons: Is a bit of a model aircraft nut, so balsa wood is always handy.

Rick Mayall: Golfing accessories.

Alfred Molina: Photos and prints relating to the *belle époque* of the transatlantic liners.

Paul Nicholas: Any of the music of Granville Bantock and Edmund Rubbra.

Michael Pennington: Fart Powder.

Siân Phillips: Indoor fireworks.

Harold Pinter: A nice mug tree from BHS.

Jonathan Pryce: Tie-dyed sweatshirts.

Corin Redgrave: Doesn't believe in all this, so just a nice

card and a big hug for good luck.

Roger Rees: Food.

Anthony Sher: Pre-war cigarette cards of footballers (but
you'll have to hunt around as he's already got a full set of
Ogden's and all the Player's series except for the rare
1927 set).

Donald Sinden: Early Left Book Club editions.

Emma Thompson: Travel Scrabble.

Zoë Wanamaker: Party novelties.

Michael York: Smart clothes.

Critics (and Those Reviews)

Personally, I have nothing against critics. I think they have an
immensely difficult job which they carry out with great
integrity, flair and, when you consider that most of them have
been heartbreakingly unsuccessful as playwrights themselves,
remarkable lack of bias. I often wish actors and directors would
spend a little less time complaining about poor reviews and
consider for a moment just how hard it must be to assess the
merits of a production and think of puns while at the same
time straining your eyes to copy out the programme notes. So
let's have a bit more tolerance please for the toilers of the
fourth estate.

Anyway, they can write whatever they like as far as I'm
concerned. It's all water off a duck's back to me because it has
always been my very strictest rule never *ever* to look at my
reviews. Not even a peek. My newsagent is bound on pain of
lingering death not to come within a hundred miles of me after
one of my first nights. Inevitably, friends will read out
particularly flattering bits on the phone but I never take any
notice, and it has never occurred to me, for instance, to have
these excerpts enlarged then take them into the bathroom,
cover them with marshmallows and roll naked on them until
I'm exhausted. What would be the point? It would be a sheer

waste of time and also rather expensive. No, steer clear of your reviews and you won't get bits of marshmallow stuck in your hair, is my advice to you.

So the question has to be asked: do we need critics at all? In my experience, audiences are an immensely intelligent group of people who are perfectly capable of making up their own minds. Similarly, actors are perfectly aware of when they are acting well and when they have been let down by bad direction and an indifferent play. And yet still these inky-fingered hacks continue to enjoy complimentary seats and full use of the office telephone afterwards. It is all very puzzling. Ho hum.

I have lost track of the number of times my name has been incorrectly spelt in the press; Michael Billington of the *Guardian* once referred to me as %icholass ¾rAig8, and some young cub on the *Mirror* came out with Nicholas Crud! All of which gives one a fair idea of just how much they really know about the theatre.

Bad reviews are bad reviews are bad reviews are bad reviews. They are occupational hazards and actors must simply accept

Often, the most constructive criticism of all comes from one's fellow actors.

them. I must confess though that when Messrs Wardle, de Jongh and Fenton saw fit to criticize my Trebonio, it afforded me the opportunity for a wry smile. I know it's a bit naughty of me to expose their ignorance in a high-profile book like this but, Gentlemen, oh Gentlemen, if you had troubled to read the play you would have realized that Trebonio is *meant* to be bad – he is a *villain*, for God's sake – you are *supposed* to be relieved when he is dead. Oh dear, I really am so very sorry for playing the character so accurately, pray forgive me Gentlemen, *mea culpa*, I shall try not to act so well in the future!

I also find it mildly flabbergasting that, when reviewing a production, critics find it necessary to drone on and on about the author (who is more often than not dead) and the play and the political implications thereof when, surely, what most people want to know about is the 'performance', the *acting*. Does it thrill? Does it stir mysterious tribal urges? Or are the actors simply making the best of inferior material? This would seem to be the one way in which the critic can make himself useful.

And so often they seem to be entirely London-minded. A friend of mine who runs the excellent Brick Kiln theatre in Wrexham had to resort to presenting a nude version of a play about Northern Ireland in order to tempt the 'qualities' up the M6. It is a very sad state of affairs indeed when critics have to be appeased in this way.

Laziness, ignorance, incompetence and all the charisma of a provincial geography master are one thing, but when the critic oversteps the boundaries of fair comment and enters the realm of personal abuse, the time has surely come to act. Bob Proudfoot was in an admittedly awful TV series: terrible direction, ghastly dialogue and poor perfs all round. Fortunately the programme has passed into oblivion and is all forgotten now, but at the time a certain so-called tabloid critic wrote: 'The leading actor (Bob Proudfoot) is about as exciting to watch as an egg-timer and as dishy as last week's washing up.

Danny La Rue's poodle has more macho magnetism and as for his face, well, it looks like a *dog's backside* [my italics] and what's more it probably smells like it too.' Now to me this is unforgivable. I regard it not only as an abuse of press freedom but as a damaging slur on a fine professional. Everyone I showed it to tried to persuade Bob to sue but he said he'd rather just forget about it and let it all blow over, which amazed me. It seemed rather ungrateful after I'd done all the photocopies and organized the Fighting Fund.

Perils of Performance

After a play has passed through the brouhaha and ballyhoo of the first night, the performances start to grow and ripen like the rarest tropical fruit in a sultan's orchard. The soft flesh of a character grows more succulent with each perf, but the fruit must never be picked. No, it must remain heavy on the bough – tempting and forbidden. Of course there is always a danger that it will over-ripen and actors must constantly guard against this – I once saw Charles Dance fall squelch all over the stage because his Harry Percy was too ripe.

There is no doubt that the theatre is a magical place where uncanny things happen. A performance can create an astounding dynamic energy. Actors who are seriously ill or suicidally depressed appear to be cured as soon as they step on to the stage. I have witnessed this phenomenon countless times, indeed it has happened to me often enough. Perhaps the most celebrated example is the case of the Victorian actor McInnerny who collapsed after a performance of *The Silver King* and was pronounced by the theatre doctor to have been clinically dead for three days.

Make no mistake, acting can be a dangerous business. Just like a thoroughbred racehorse, the actor who has reached full 'performance fitness' is susceptible to a number of mental and physical problems, some of which can cause him to break down completely. Little do audiences know the kinds of risks the actor runs in performance. He treads a tightrope – the more agile and breathtaking his steps, the closer he comes to disaster. Here are a few of the problems which can strike a first-class actor at any time:

Actoplasm – When an actor is really 'on song', a substance builds up inside his mouth and is discharged with every percussive or dental consonant. The substance is known as *Actoplasm* and it can be very unpleasant for the other performers and the first three rows of the audience.

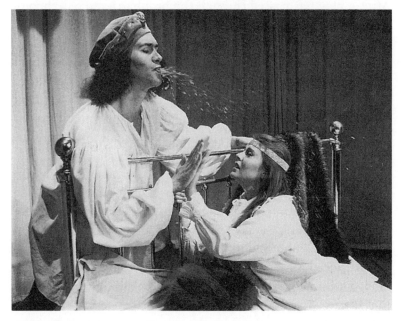

Actoplasm.

Enactulatio Praecox – All actors find this a very embarrassing one. Put simply, it is a premature eruption of emotion. It mainly affects young, over-eager actors. Most old pros know how to hold it back until their final entrance, but it can happen to the best of us. Nothing worse than letting everything go in Sc. 1 – where do you go from there?

Perforgasm – Rather difficult to explain in layman's terms but, basically, it is a 'performer-audience empathy overload'. The effect is to make the sufferer the focus of attention for the duration of the attack. *Perforgasm* has been called 'the selfish complaint' because of its side-effects, but theories that it only strikes an actor when his agent is 'in' are grossly unfair.

Truthpumping – Although not an acting injury in itself, it is such a very dangerous practice that I have included it. There are times when an actor needs to attack a speech or scene with an extra burst of energy; for instance, when inferior dialogue or poor direction are allowing the audience's attention to wander. The actor literally pumps himself into a kind of acting overdrive or 'superformance'. Many of us use this technique often enough, BUT you really have to know what you're about, and of course you must be super-fit.

The risks to the inexperienced are enormous; torn muscles and spears are commonplace, and I have seen false noses and moustaches flying off like clay pigeons as young tyros have striven to engage the audience. I have seen ripping flannels and blazer buttons fizzing out over the stalls like dum-dum bullets. I have seen ruptures, black-outs and one terrible fatality at the Westminster Theatre.

So the rule with *Truthpumping* is, 'If in doubt, *don't*'.

Perf-quaking – Very awkward indeed, this one. When the actor senses a surge in the audience's response to what he is doing, the neuro-motors are liable to go into spasm. Once spasm has occurred, he will begin to make violent physical movements. Eventually, he will lose control completely and have to be held down.

Perf-quaking. 'Eventually, he will lose control completely and have to be held down.'

Enactulatio Praecox at the Mermaid, 1972.

Miss Pauline Collins reaching *Perforgasm.*

Superformance. Merrison is overwhelmed by the size of his part.

Actaplaning – Very much frowned upon in the subsidized sector of the profession these days.

By switching off the emotional generator, slipping one hand into the trouser pocket and latching on to a tennis racket or champagne glass with the other, it is possible to *Actaplane* through some plays quite successfully. The *danger* with *Actaplaning* is that in the event of a mishap (french window jamming, phone not ringing, perky maid failing to enter with telegram), one is likely to be very badly thrown and run off through the fireplace.

Blow-out – I had rather hoped I would not have to write about this since I have a superstitious aversion even to saying the word. But here goes. *Blow-out* is quite simply the worst thing that can happen to an actor. Basically, *Blow-out* is the point you reach when you are acting so well that you cannot act any more. First there is a tingling in the toes, the heart pounds, there is a power-surge like the kick of a mule and the next thing you see is the solemn face of the stage manager as you come to on the dressing-room couch.

Peter O'Toole was once thought to have blown out, but it proved to be an unusually long pause.

One hears some astonishing confidential admissions from colleagues about their own personal acting weak points. You would no doubt be amazed to learn the true identities of some of these poor suffering loves, but professional loyalty compels me to use impenetrable code-names.

Ian McKellenford cannot truthfully play an arthritic Norwegian for longer than an act and a half without completely falling back on technique, while Albert Finneystein has nightmares about playing Chekhov on an apron stage. Charles Dancehall, the silly old noddle, wouldn't know a Brechtian image-cluster if it leapt out of his filofax and tried to shave his stubble off, and if you've ever wondered why

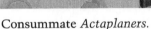
Consummate *Actaplaners.*

Blow-out! Diana can do nothing for Keith.

Sir Alec Guinnessisgood-for you avoided appearing in farces by Ray Cooney – skimpy calves is the answer to that one.

Poor sausages. How I feel for them. How we actors suffer. Let no one get hold of the idea that being a piece of human litmus paper is easy.

I shudder to mention my own particular bugbear. It is something I would not wish on my worst enemy. It is this: I'm on-stage, saying the lines, thinking the thoughts, getting right under the skin of the character when suddenly – whoosh – there I am in Leicester in 1324, or in Regency Bath or in Krakow in 1951. The energy of concentration is so strong you see, that my mind becomes a sort of time machine – an *Actardis*. It is an absolute nightmare. It stalks me like an albatross and I'm sure it has taken years off my life.

To pick a random instance, I was doing a matinee of *The Cuckolde of Leicester* at Stratford and had just started the scene where I unwittingly eat the severed head of my twin brother, Falseface. As I turned out front to deliver the 'This

Pasha's top my hunger will assuage' speech, I thought I heard birdsong. Suddenly the auditorium seemed to be filled with brilliant sunlight. Before me stood a milling throng of noisy playgoers in buckram and fustian. In the pit a wench was selling oranges, swifts darted around the wooden turrets, flags fluttered high above us and I caught a whiff of wood-smoke from a brazier somewhere in the lane outside the original Globe theatre – for this, as you will have realized, was where my *Actardis* had transported me.

I continued the speech and seemed to cope quite effortlessly with the backchat of the swains in the galleries and the chaff of the groundlings pressed hard by the front of the stage. Normally I'm a hopeless ad-libber, but when a wealthy merchant called out, 'Eat not that head!' it seemed the most natural thing in the world to reply, 'Woulds't have your Truepate starve, Gentles?' and wink rudely at two noble-women in a stage box before picking up the thread of the text.

I am told that when I came off-stage I bellowed to the stage management for sack and griddle cakes. Apparently I even tried to organize a boar-hunt in the canteen.

But perhaps the most nightmarish of all the *Actardis's* sudden bursts of activity happened when I was in the BBC cashier's office trying to get my expenses for an *I Claudius* I was doing. One minute I was in the queue minding my own business, then suddenly – whoosh – there I was speaking in Latin hexameters and trying to disembowel a cleaner.

I have had to endure the curse of the *Actardis* now for *SEVEN BLOODY YEARS!*

There are many more such crises which can afflict actors – *Actaclysm, Phantom Blow-out, Soliloquaking* – the list is terrifyingly long. It was to try to remedy them that the wise and wonderful Cis Pissdt opened her Acting Clinic at Stratford in the mid-Sixties.

Cis has certainly been the strongest influence on my career to date, and over the last twenty-five years she has become the spiritual leader of hundreds of actors everywhere. She is a truly remarkable person, and she must be the only guru to smoke eighty a day and wear cavalry twill trousers with a poncho. She has taught me so much – found notes in my voice and muscles in my instrument that I could not have believed existed. I suppose this book is in many ways a love letter to Cis, although if I told her that, she would no doubt dismiss it with the customary string of obscenities, followed by a request for a barley wine and a strange sort of rasping noise.

I first went to the Clinic in 1970 when I was in a show called *Totally Free London*. I didn't have many lines in the play (it was more a sort of mime/ballet actually) but I somehow kept sliding into my vowels from the left instead of taking them from behind in the proper way, and I felt that a few sessions with Cis might lick the voice into shape. I'll never forget the first time I saw her, she was in her kitchen, warming up with Michael Hordern (later Sir Michael of course). Her hands were under his back and she was heaving away, trying to get him to

Totally Free London. *1970 (NC third from left).*

make full use of the diaphragm. Anyway, after her session with Mikey was over, she sat me down, looked into my voice box and sighed heavily. When I regained consciousness he told me that there was a great deal of work to be done. She still says the same thing after thirty years, but the progress we have made in that time is immeasurable. Her formidable appearance – the wild silver hair and the calloused toes peeping through the sandals – belies the gentle way she handles the young. I'll never forget her sensitive treatment of Julie Walter's *Premature eruption,* and the way she nursed Richard Griffiths through his first *Blow-out* is a legend in the profession.

It would be no exaggeration to say that she has rescued some actors' careers from disaster. In the mid-Seventies Bill Wackerbath kept on *Hypervibrating.* He was in despair as to how to remedy the problem. He had tried hypnotism, acupuncture, herbal remedies; finally he went to Cis. Screwing in her monocle, she looked at him thoughtfully. After a few seconds she diagnosed a displaced dactyl and, without even removing the Craven 'A' from her lips, she punched him hard between the shoulder-blades and told him to bugger off. He had no more trouble from that day on.

She spotted Harriet Rackstraw's *Blow-out anxiety complex* even before Hat had become properly aware of it. Donald Sinden is always round there having a diphthong lanced or something. Her humming exercises have made the explosive bilabial a thing of the past.

Thanks to Cis, young actors are more aware of their coccyxes than at any other point in history. In an episode of *Dallas* the other night, I noticed an actress use her vertebrae in a way that was straight out of one of Cis's manuals. Her influence in all the acting media has been enormous. Anthony Hopkins, Peter O'Toole and Michael Elphick are all Pissdt actors, and many leading directors regard her books as holy writ. *The Elastic Actor* is the vade mecum of a whole generation of actors who came through in the Sixties.

*Cis Pissdt's
Acting Clinic.*

Though a little bad-tempered these days, Cis continues to run the Clinic with the same combative energy as always. She is a true original and, it goes without saying, one of the most important figures in post-war osteo-vocal awareness. Perhaps it would be appropriate to end this chapter with one of her favourite expressions: 'Here endeth the fucking lesson, darling.'

5

Brass Tacks

'Anyone who thinks acting is easy hasn't seen the armpits of my War Requiem dress' – Tilda Swinton

Out of Work

An actor cannot work unless he is employed to do so. A painter can paint, a writer can write, an Inland Revenue clerk can go off and do some auditing whenever the fancy takes him, but without a contract of employment, an actor is 'out of work'. A lame gazelle, a firework on November 7th, a puncture repair outfit in Peru before the arrival of Pizarro. He is, in short, available.

Yes, it *is* bloody hard, one *is* desperate, one is suicidal, but one must always remember that one *is* an actor.

In the last few years I have been in the fortunate position of having *too much* work, which is lovely, but I remember only too clearly the pain, sweat, heartbreak and sheer bloody misery of unemployment. 'O inactivitas misere mea!' Other actors who have not been as lucky as me (because luck does come into it – a lot) might be interested in these few tips on how to cope with being 'out of work'.

Keeping the Instrument in Tune

It is essential to keep your instrument – yourself – supple in between engagements. Voice and body exercises are the best way of doing this. First of all, here are some noises you can make in those idle moments down at the Job Centre or in the bus queue.

Me-Me-Me-Me-Me-Me-Meeeeeeeeee-Me-Me-Me-Me.

Me-my-mo. Me-my-ma. Me-my-mum. Mummy-mummy.

Waaaaaaaaaaaaaaaaaaaaaa-wah.

Up and down the lift shaft bounced the Spanish dwarf (repeat)

And now some positions for you to get into. You can do these at home or in the gym, but don't rush into it. Take it gently to begin with.

1. Holding the coffee in the right hand, raise the left arm.
2. Now pass the coffee to the left hand and raise the right arm.
3. Probably best to the put coffee down now, and raise both arms.

Filling in

If you can't face the Job Centre, there are any number of jobs available to the inACTive actor:

1. Moss Bros: A long-term commitment. Ideal for pantomime artists, and perks can be good. For the relief of the out-of-work-job blues, there is nothing quite like sending an American off to Ascot in a dinner jacket.

2. Extra work: Don't touch it. You might know some of the actors in the cast.

3. Decorating your agent's office: The best of the lot. You are on the spot to suggest yourself for parts. Your very presence is a testament to their inefficiency.

4. TV ratings researcher: Standing all day in the high street asking people what they watched last night is hard on the feet. Falsification of forms, however, can bring enormous benefits. It is rumoured that the second series of *This Life* was a direct consequence of the cast's tireless efforts up and down Oxford Street.

5. Alternative cabaret: Comedy is pretty well sewn up these days but there is still a *modest* living to be earned as a 'speciality' act. Call yourself after a cleaning fluid, pull a pair of Y-fronts over your head and juggle with *one* ping-pong ball.

6. Teaching at RADA: You have to have a bit of a name to do this but it can be a real peach of a job. Just send the little bastards off to the zoo, then it's feet up with the crossword.

7. Backstage work:
Dresser: Very popular in the days immediately following the abolition of the Lord Chamberlain's Office but the job is more demanding nowadays.
NB: Avoid the Haymarket – there is no tannoy and the stairs are a nightmare.
Stagehand: Worst show to work on – *Phantom of the Opera* (original Victorian stage machinery).
Best show – *The Mousetrap* (one set and a telly with Sky in the crew room).

8. The final solution: Mini-cab driving.

The Twilight Zone

There is a sort of halfway house between unemployment and employment. It is called the Fringe. Largely unknown to the general public, it takes place in pubs and community centres up and down the country. Unemployed actors choose a play then get their friends to come and see them perform it. It is a marvellous way of meeting dear old mates again, and exposing the cruelty of mill-owners in 1860. I love the Fringe.

'Clever Old You! Who Else is in It?'

Let us assume that you have now got a job. You have agreed the money, read the script and are ready to start rehearsals. Here are a few hints on how to get through the period of engagement with minimum fuss and maximum advantage:

The Director: A director can be your closest ally or your bitterest enemy, it all depends on whether or not it was his idea to cast you. If it was the author's or the management's, then you are almost certainly in for trouble.

Destroying the Director: It is an irrefutable fact that a director must be pushed to the verge of mental breakdown before he is able to do his best work. Everyone in the cast must do their bit to destroy his peace of mind. Be difficult if he tries to cut any of your lines, *pop out* to the newsagent just before he needs you for a scene, *ring him up* late at night and *complain* about the other actors spoiling your best moments, *grind* him down.

The Very Worst Sin: If you happen to be late for rehearsals, don't just say, 'Sorry,' and slink off to a chair until you are needed, tell everyone precisely *why* you are late. Unless you explain about the traffic, or the cat making ominous noises or the tube being stuck in a tunnel, they will simply think you have overslept. If you fail to be meticulously honest with your colleagues in

Production meeting at Windsor Rep, 1987.

rehearsal, how can you hope to present the naked truth on stage?

Creating the Right Impression: Try to get friends to ring you up at the rehearsal room. It is always good to be 'in demand'. Wear a bleeper if it helps.

Good Company Feeling: It is very important that actors stick together in a company, encouraging and cherishing each other's rare talents. If an actor is giving a bad performance, you must never let him know it. Say something friendly along the lines of 'I think what you're doing is very brave,' or 'You're absolutely marvellous as —, don't you listen to what anyone else is saying.' And if there is an actor in the cast who is unpopular or just a bad mixer, you should never mock him openly. By all means invent little signs and code-words between yourselves so that you can enjoy giggling at him when he is not looking, but you must *never* let him see what is going on.

Nerves: You will often find an older actor in the bar before a per-formance getting steadily nervous. Sometimes, he can get so nervous that he will stumble and slur his words. When Bill Wackerbath played Brutus he was completely nervous most nights. I've seen Bob Proudfoot nervous as a newt but still brilliant.

Rehearsal Etiquette: When you are delving down below the earth's crust in search of the searing truth of a character, it is inevitable that you will sometimes forget your lines. When this occurs the proper expression is, 'It's awfully difficult to concentrate when people are moving about. Now, where was I?' or alternatively, 'Is that chair supposed to be there? It's rather throwing.'

When chatting to your fellow actors, always adopt a jovial tone and, whenever possible, an amusing accent.

Rehearsal Expressions to Take You Through the Day

Section 1: Arrival

Line	Accent	Gesture
Mornin' Jim Lad, aha, ooh arr . . .	*West Country*	*Screw up left eye and stand on one leg.*
Top o' the marnin' to yer, Pathrick . . .	*Irish*	*Tug forelock.*
Bonjour mon vieux, hee-hon, hee-hon, hee-hon...	*French*	*Wave arms about.*
Awright John.	*Cockney*	*Stick chin out. Rotate shoulders.*

A few simple 'hellos':

Harrow	*Chinese*	*Narrow eyes and bow slowly.*
Hollothurrrrr	*Scottish*	*(No gesture needed)*
Hellayow	*Upper Class*	*Royal wave.*

The well-made play.

Section 2: The Pre-Lunch Period

'Now, shall I have a cup of coffee? That's the burning issue of the moment.'

'My agent said Channel 5 would make a difference but I haven't had a sausage since before Christmas, mind you I happen to know I'm on a BBC blacklist and voiceovers are a closed book unless you happen to be called Angus Deayton. Ho-hum twiddly-dee, we survive.'

'Methinks the nibbling hour approacheth.'

Section 3: The Post-Lunch Period

'Shall we wander back?'

'This job is costing me money, what with the fares and the meals out.'

'Are they going to get to our bit this year, do you think?'

'I feel another cake coming on.'

Section 4: Departure.

'Och well, home again, home again, jiggety-jig.'

'Cheery bye-bye.'

'Hi-ho, 'tis the wending hour. The Chiswick High Road beckoneth.'

Research

Long before the grind of rehearsal comes the sweat of research. There are no hard and fast rules governing how one carries out this slog, one simply has to follow one's own in-built acting Geiger counter.

It is often helpful to simulate the conditions under which your character will have to exist. For instance it is well known in the business that before filming the series *Unexploded Bomb*, Nick Berry tested his courage with fireworks, and I don't think I'm giving away any trade secrets when I say that Charles Dance gets ideas for some of his startling portrayals by leafing through back numbers of *The Yachtsman* to get exactly the right kind of smouldering expression. My own researches for Foppishness began with a weekend break in Bath, while with Truepate it was mainly physical preparation; hour after hour of crouching, limping and jumping off rostra. But the important thing is to keep one's eyes open, you never know when you're going to see something useful, something that will set the Geiger counter bleeping like a Jap's wristwatch in a quiet bit. The melancholy gait of a traffic warden, the cheery whistle of the butcher's boy, a freshly tossed salad.

My old mucker, Ben Kingsley, and I were chatting over a pint once and I asked him what it was that gave him the key to his Oscar-winning characterization of Gandhi.

'Now you won't believe this, Nick,' he said, 'but it was a piece of piss. As soon as the kecks were off, I knew I'd got the bastard.'

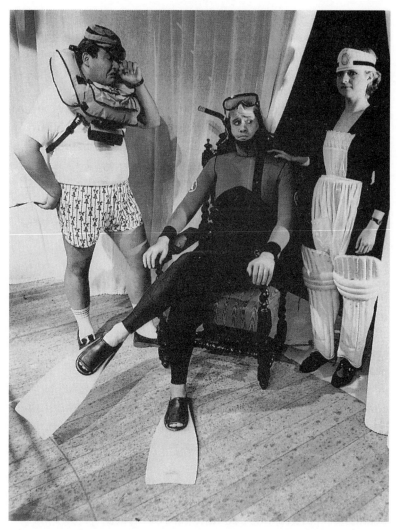

Robert Lepage's production of The Winslow Boy *(Der Unterwasserkammer Theater, Berlin, 1999).*

Of course, on film one can often get away with a great deal less research than would be required by a really discerning theatre audience. But having said that, Ben was wonderful.

Indeed, clothing can make an enormous difference to one's

performance and can often help to break an 'acting block'. Nigel Havers has often found the regimental tie to be an absolute Godsend in this respect; with Hordern's Lear it was the cardigan, while Ronald Pickup has always been a confirmed sock man.

Anthony Sher has not been slow to appropriate what I regard as my most valuable research technique, namely drawing mountains. By sketching out the nuances and flavours of a character, often in a simplistic abstract way, I must have stacked up enough 'performance volts' to run the Piccadilly Line for a year.

Opposite are some examples of my work in this vital area.

My Tool

Just as a painter must keep his brushes clean and a safe-cracker must ensure that his gelignite will work and a judge must look after his wig, so must an actor take great care of his tool. His arms, his legs, his ribcage, his coccyx are essential pieces of professional equipment – his livelihood. Nicholas Craig is not just a famous face and an inscription on an award, he is a complete tool as well. I see so many actors ill-treating their tools and draining their emotional fire-power by raising families and looking after elderly relatives and I think to myself, 'What *are* they doing?'

I lead a pretty riotous and anarchic life, what with my late-night suppers and my regular Sunday morning 'Boules 'n' Beaujolais' parties, but I do take care of myself.

My mammoth walks across London keep me in peak condition. I walk absolutely everywhere. I never catch a bus, seldom take a train and I think I would rather be executed than go on the tube.

I especially like walking across London at night. I love the people of the night, you see: the pimps, the prostitutes, the winos. They're free, like actors. As we pass, we exchange sly

The Jungfrau – Hamlet.

Box Hill – Romeo.

Table Mountain – Coriolanus.

The Urals – Prince Hal.

looks as if to say, 'Mortgages? Pension schemes? No. Not quite us, I think.'

I am the despair of all my friends. 'Please, please, Nick,' they chorus, 'just for once, take a cab!' But I never do. I walk. I once worked out that if I live to be seventy-five, I will have walked to Saturn and back four times.

Some of my walks have been extraordinarily long and interesting – but, oh dear, I feel a digression coming on.

The legendary Henry Irving was another great walker and there is a gorgeous anecdote about him taking a stroll down The Strand with Ellen Terry. 'Sir Henry', as he had just become (although he was always The Guv'nor to those who worked with him), had decided to take the morning off (the first time he had done so, it was said, for thirty-five years).

'To think, Nell,' he piped, as they passed the recently refurbished Tivoli theatre (originally built in 1890) at a spanking clip, 'a Knight of the Realm at last, and I only mmmmm a poor parson's son.'

Whereupon, who should saunter into view but none other than Herbert Beerbohm Tree. The two great actor-managers had no alternative but to greet each other. (They had not spoken, of course, since a disagreement in a chop house over the rights to the play *Nan o' Ninepence* twenty-eight years previously.)

'It is mmmmm a fine morning, Gaffer,' trilled Irving, deliberately using Tree's old nickname (after 1899 it was proper to address him as The Admiral).

'Indeed it ahhhhh indeed it is,' rumbled Tree, who was thought to have some Jewish blood, 'and all the finer for seeing you, Bo'sun.' (A sobriquet abandoned by Irving after the first night of *The Bells*, as Tree well knew.) Then he produced some embroidery which he had done, he asserted, with the help of the future Queen Mary.

'What on *earth* fff-ffffuff is *that*?' rasped The Archduke of the boards, inimitably.

'I think it's his lunch chdm-chdm-chdm,' said Ellen Terry,

The designer strikes.

the mother of Edward Gordon Craig and grand-aunt of the as yet unborn John Gielgud, with impeccable sang froid.

History does not relate what The Guv'nor said but his face must have been a picture.

Sweet little anecdote, isn't it? Anyway, as I was saying, despite being a workaholic I do look after myself. As an actor I have to.

Walking keeps the joints and muscles of my instrument in tip-top order, but the actor also needs a high degree of spiritual suppleness. That I have managed to remain so emotionally agile over the last few gruelling years is mainly due to my discovery of the ancient and absolutely fascinating oriental art of K'Dang.

K'Dang is a total mind body release/defence, breathing/ movement system designed to free the body's release/defence mechanisms and realize more fully the individual's breathing potential space/time quotient. The emphasis is very much on breathing. On inhaling, we are encouraged to think of *drawing in* air, and on exhaling we are encouraged to think of *releasing it*. The whole exercise is, if you analyse it, one of the simplest forms of activity there is. It is absolutely ideal for actors.

My K'Dangi (teacher), Roger Elroy Jenkins Ho, believes that we must unlearn all the received wisdom about breathing before we can adopt the way of K'Dang. He calls it 'getting rid of all the crap'. The process is long, frustrating and fairly expensive.

My friends often ask me why I am so utterly dedicated to this ancient art, what it is that makes me drive right to the other side of town to stand facing a church-hall wall hour after punishing hour, Thursday night after Thursday night. I simply refer them to my record of work over the last few years. I have simply never stopped. Fingers crossed it will continue.

K'Dang has made me a whole person it has influenced my life and work immeasurably. When I was in *Lord Algernon's Country Retreat*, critics wrote that they had never seen a Bertie so plangent with the wisdom of the Orient. My decision to play Bertie in full K'Dangli trousers, duri and dakiri was obviously a factor but it was the inner strength of my K'Dang which gave the performance its hypnotic power.

Awful Things That Can Happen

It always absolutely astonishes me and makes me fall over backwards in complete amazement that some young actors appear not to want to go into weekly rep. When I first entered the profession, I couldn't wait to go into weekly rep at places like Kettering and Oadby and Ashton-under-Lyme. Unfortunately there weren't any theatres there, which was an enormous disappointment to me personally, as an actor. But I did go to Fishguard which was marvellous.

The dry.

Apart from one infamous occasion when it wasn't quite so marvellous.

I was doing a *Most Foul* at Fishguard, and halfway through Act Two the worst happened. I dried absolutely stone cold dead. Panic. Tony, bless him, hurtled on to help me out – bringing the stage left wall with him as he entered. Not only had he forgotten, in his haste, to take his snow shoes off but he had also omitted to pick up the gun. We ad-libbed frantically as the set came crashing down around us, and after much confusion I ended up having to murder myself with an envelope. We tried to make it as moving and truthful as possible, but I remember thinking at the time, 'I wonder what the good burghers of Fishguard will make of this!'

When the auditorium caved in we thought, 'Oh well, that's it. We've lost them.'

But the extraordinary thing is that when I went to pull my landlady out of the rubble, I looked at her face, and you know what? She was weeping.

That's the power of the theatre for you.

Hilarious Things That Can Happen

How I loved my time at Thirsk. We did a different play every fortnight and, I can tell you, some pretty hilarious things used to happen. I remember once when we were performing *A Little House on the Coast* in the evening and rehearsing *Seaside Bungalow* in the day; Digby Farquharson, who was playing the Gordon Harker part in *Little House*, came on for the drinks scene in Act One wearing his *Bungalow* socks!! It was all we could do to stop ourselves from bursting into uncontrollable giggles, which would have been very unprofessional. Somehow, we managed to get ourselves out of it by ad-libbing, and not a soul in the audience realized what had happened. Great days. I don't suppose we shall see them again.

Emergency Lines

An hour spent committing these to memory will save you a hundred hours of excruciating embarrassment.

Where are they, the bastards?

'I'll just go and check if there are any murderers outside.'

'Et tu iterum, Cassius?' (And you again, Cassius?) 'Ubique procreatus Brute?' (Where the fuck is Brutus?)

'When shall I meet the other two again?'

'Westmoreland comes late upon the hour, methinks I'll take mine ease behind yon wall until he do approach.'

Oh no, pissed again!

'Mark ye how the King is sore distracted by affairs of state and cannot stand.'

'Your burps inform me ye would as lief be damned to hell as see me crowned. Nay, I'll not fight with thee. See, with my own usurper's sword I slay myself.'

'Methinks the noble Lord would impart the news from France, which I'll wager is as follows . . .'

You'd better bloody buy me a pint afterwards.

'Though ye say naught, thy visage tells me ye would exile me to France.'

'I can see in your eyes, m'lud, that you mean me to be taken from here to a place of execution, where I shall be hanged by the neck until I am dead. But I didn't do it, d'you hear? I'm innocent, damn you!'

'Perchance my Lord Hamlet is wondering whether or not it is all worth it. Whether 'tis nobler in the mind . . .' (and so on, as far as necessary)

Damn! It's in the dressing-room.

'Would great Caesar vouchsafe me his dagger for a moment?'

'And thus, with this poisoned empty scabbard, I do end my miserable life.'

'Why then, we'll fight with shields alone!'

Bloody props!

'Aha. The silencer works perfectly.'

'It's one of those new phones with a very quiet ring.'

'I've got a gun that works out in the car, damn you. Come with me and I'll shoot you like a dog!'

'Ho! Bring me a dishcloth and another draught of poison.'

It's stuck!

Never mind, Algy, we can easily get to the garden through the fireplace.'

'Cynthia! I thought you were in Paris. Have you been listening up the chimney all this time?'

'Look here, I'm sick of Champagne. Let's celebrate this happy day by shaking hands instead.'

Fringe Crises.

'So what if the pram's empty! There's another baby behind the sofa. Let's eat that one instead!'

'Bloody men! Typical of them to manufacture a kettle that won't boil.'

The multiple dry.

6

Around the World
in Eighty Plays

Peter Brook's D'ik

'Why not have everyone swinging about on trapezes?' I had said to Peter in a cold rehearsal room one morning in 1970.

'What, *all* of them?' Peter had replied incredulously. 'Puck? Titania? Bottom?'

'Yes, and the Lovers. You know – swinging about.'

'I suppose we could give it a try, Nick,' he had said, thoughtfully popping a Sweetex into his coffee. And the rest, as they say, is history.

As a relatively junior member of that company (I was understudying Toadflax, as a matter of fact) it was immensely gratifying to see a suggestion of mine have such an enormous impact on World Theatre. The production is always referred to as 'Brook's Dream', which is quite right since he was the director and no one was more delighted than I at the plaudits which were lavished upon that wise, slightly balding head. Naturally, Peter was tremendously grateful to me for putting him on the theatrical map, so to speak, and I knew it would only be a short time before we were working together again.

I read with great interest about his move to Paris and his search for an internationally accessible narrative form. Clearly this was a product of the discussions we had had during those early *Dream* rehearsals. Remarkably, he was following an almost identical path to me in his development as an artist. I had to be with him.

'I'm coming out,' I told him when I eventually got through to his *atelier*. He made all sorts of protestations about not having a suitable 'biggy' for me, but I swept them aside and, within twenty-four hours of putting the phone down, I was standing in a disused abattoir in the *10ième arrondissement* daubing myself with mud.

Oh, what a door was opened to me that first morning! Here, at long last, was the kind of theatre I had been seeking: primal, epic story-telling in humble classless surroundings; a theatre for everyone. It was exhilarating, liberating. I was discovering my inner-storyteller; Nicholas Craig the gipsy pedlar of spells and dreams; the vagabond troubadour who takes life as he finds it and bites his thumb at danger; the *beau chevalier* who dines with the Duchess and laughs with the scullion and probably beds the pair of them; the gay dog who hunts with the Bishop and brawls with the tar; the singer of songs, the clown, the dark-eyed illusionist. It didn't matter at all when some tramps told me that I had got the wrong derelict building, for I had discovered something infinitely more precious – I had discovered Nicholas Craig the Global Artist.

Peter seemed surprised but obviously delighted to see me when I arrived at his office and he broke off a conversation he was having in Manx with a Tamil actor to give me big hugs. It was the first time we had met since the *Dream* and I think we were both a bit weepy. We talked in broad terms of how our ideas had developed over the last few years and I could see that he was bursting to tell me about his latest project.

It was to be an adaptation of the ancient Indonesian legend *D'ikwi Ting-ton*. I was immediately seized with enthusiasm and bombarded Peter with questions about stylistic approach, ritual catharsis formulae and whether he had cast the main part yet.

He shrugged his shoulders. 'All I've got at this stage, Nick, is a wonderful group of internationally talented actors and four hundredweight of potting compost. The project could go in any direction. It is very, *very* exciting.'

There was no doubt that Brook had assembled a remarkable array of talent (living proof – if it were needed – that China has its Peter Bowleses just as Hungary boasts its Googie Witherses). There were Swiss, Kiwis, Derrymen – all tremendously exciting. There was an immaculate Solomon Islander very much in the Nigel Patrick mould and several Faeroese actors who would, frankly, make the current RSC crop look like a bunch of amateurs. Then there was a half-Finnish, half-Madagascan actor who could do things with a bone which brought tears to your eyes. There were Bretons, Springboks, Walloons and a wonderful gamin Prussian. I palled up with a Pathan lass who shared my passion for Victorian chamber-pots.

Peter conducted the early rehearsals with painstaking thoroughness. There were language difficulties of course – it once took him thirty-five minutes to say 'Coffee-time, girls and boys' in ways that everyone could understand – but we were soon producing some immensely interesting work. It was a time of stripping off our preconceptions and revealing our emotional nudity to each other. Using gravel and feathers, we were learning to explore and love ourselves all over again – to re-love ourselves. It was tremendously stimulating, though rather messy of course.

In order to be truly international, and to be understood by our simple peasant audiences the world over, we invented a completely new language in which to perform the *D'ik*. It was composed of Church Latin, Persian, Welsh and Maori. We called it Horghczitt and within a few months we were jabbering away to each other like natives. Horghczitt had a strange poetry all of its own and it suited the primal myth perfectly when the Narrator stepped out of his mud mound and

'I invented as never before.'

delivered the first line, 'Ha-lo k'Ids. Hav agoo d'Krismus diju?' the effect was electric.

I was playing the Bird of Paradise, whom D'ik meets on his travels to the South Seas. No wings, no Kirby wire, just a cardboard beak, a feather and my talent. I invented as never before, preening, strutting, having baths and doing my best to avoid the sudden assaults of Brunhilde who was playing the cat.

There was a big set-piece scene at the end of Part Four in which D'ik dreams of his homeland and his sweetheart, the daughter of the wicked Al-Damahn Fitswahan. He imagines his helpless love searching the countryside for him, wailing as she does so, 'Nien myls fromlon don-ands tilnoh syn of D'ik.' It was a very moving section and of course it was vital that it should work properly. But no matter how much energy we put into it, it still seemed curiously lifeless. What the trouble was we couldn't tell. Peter ordered a month's meditation in Kashmir but when we came back it was no better. Then, one day in about the eighth month of rehearsal, Peter came up with a typically international and innovative approach to the problem. Just before we began to play the scene for the umpteenth time he stopped us and said simply, 'Do nothing.'

I twigged immediately but some of the others were a bit slow to comprehend the maestro. 'Faites rien,' he continued, 'ποιετε ονδεν . . . Ddoliog nos,' etc. At the end of the day we tried it. We actually *did nothing* – and it was the most exciting moment I have ever had in a disused abattoir. Fifteen of us standing there doing absolutely bugger-all and it was riveting.

Suddenly the show was in terrific shape, all that remained was to find some simple mountain peasants to perform it to. We scoured Montmartre but nary a one could we find. Then there was the additional snag that Peter would only allow the *D'ik* to be performed on the south side of a volcano at dawn during Ramadan. So our joy over the brilliance of the production was tempered by the knowledge that our chances of performing it were steadily receding.

Peter found the Mexican and Javanese arts councils to be entirely unhelpful in the matter of a venue, while the Neapolitans, predictably, wanted to make all kinds of idiotic conditions. We spent several tense weeks in Paris practising cries and squawks while Peter jetted further and further afield in search of somewhere to put his *D'ik*. And all the time Ramadan was getting closer.

Finally, the message came telling us to get ourselves on a plane to Iceland asap. The newly formed volcanic island of Surtesy was, Peter said, the perfect setting. As for the audience, he had found a small community in the Cahchapoyas region of Peru who were as poor and unsophisticated as they were desperate for good theatre. He had made arrangements for the entire village to be flown out to Reykjavik.

He was right about the setting. Apart from some rather dry acoustics, there was no doubt that the *D'ik* had found its spiritual home. The day before the performance we busied ourselves mixing up the special muds and improvising good luck prezzies out of pumice.

At three a.m. on March 23rd 1981, the first and only performance of the *D'ik* began. At four a.m. we heard the news that the Peruvian peasants' charter flight was grounded at Luxembourg. But it didn't matter because at five p.m. the following day the sun sank behind the volcano and the audience, consisting of Nicholas de Jongh, the crew of a herring trawler and a girl from *Time Out*, wept openly. There was no question that Peter Brook's *D'ik* was the theatrical event of the decade.

It will always be my proudest boast that I was a vital element in that extraordinary mixture of Horghczitt, mud and international talent. It is a tragic reflection of the state of the world theatre now that not a single nation possessing an area of high vulcanicity has come forward to fund another performance.

Grotowski, and the Work of the Wroclaw Theatre Laboratory

To discuss fully the influence of Jerzy Grotowski on my work, and vice versa, would be impossible even in a book fourteen times as long as this, although exactly how long this one is going to be is not something I appear to have any say in. First of all one is told that there are only going to be sixty pictures, then it's, 'Oh dear, but we don't think there's going to be room for all your poems,' (some of which were written specially for this book), and 'Oh, do we really need the comprehensive record of your dreams since 1977?' I mean, I am asked to write about my life and my thoughts on the theatre and yet when I dutifully provide this material I am told that it is no longer required. I wonder if they actually want me to write anything at all or whether they would rather have just a few blank pages and a picture of me on the cover so that they can use my name to sell it. Oh yes, and the latest on the launch by the way is that the present publishers, in their wonderful magnanimity, have deigned to offer to pay for the wine – if I do the food. I wouldn't mind making the food (and I would certainly do it a great deal better than some gaggle of Sloane caterers who use mayonnaise out of a jar), but I'm buggered if I'm going to spend two days killing myself in the kitchen (which still isn't properly finished yet), only to have my quiches and dips washed down with some terrible medium-sweet Château Plonk. And it's the principle involved. Why the bloody hell should I? The thing is, of course, they know I'm easy-going, they know I don't make a fuss about things, and they are simply trying to take advantage of me. Well, I'm sorry but 'so far and no further'. So, 'No', actually.

Poor Theatre: a Reappraisal

I mean, just *little* things, like this morning, when I rang up to speak to the Managing Editor about an idea I had for the cover – 'in a meeting'. Well *why* was he in a meeting? If I'm in a play in the West End, it's no good me sending some bint from South Ken on to the stage to say, 'Sorry, audience, Mr Craig is in a meeting. Would you like to come back and try again in a couple of hours?' So then I asked if I could speak to Lucinda – 'on holiday'. Finally got through to Candida who blithely tells me she hasn't even approached the *Observer* about serialization on the front page of the Review. I suppose it's common sense really, I mean we wouldn't want to start encouraging people to buy the book – they might read it! They might even, heaven forbid, *enjoy* it!

No, I mustn't think about it or I'll just get cross. Best move on to something else. But really!

The Silver Screen

And it's not as though one were being paid vast sums exactly. No, stop it Craig. Onwards and upwards, end of moan.

There is a famous story told about a certain American actor making some big epic film or other. Needless to say, the gentleman was a devotee of the much-vaunted Method (it is said that for his earlier role in *Jelly Man* he had all his bones surgically broken). The character he was playing in this particular film was required to commit suicide and he went to incredible lengths to get himself into the right state of mind for the crucial scene; he went around smashing up bars and crashing cars and he even invested heavily in a fringe theatre company.

Eventually, the day came to shoot the scene. Now a number of English actors had been brought in to lend weight and tone to the production, and they began to get somewhat impatient when friend Yankee-Doodle held up shooting for most of the morning, protesting, in his East Side twang, that he couldn't quite 'feel it' yet.

'Ever thought of *acting*, ducky?' said Benny Kingsley, with impeccable delivery.

'Look love, just say the lines and try not to bump into the furniture,' chimed in Podge Bates.

'Hurry up, chummy,' said Freddie Molina, 'I want to get to the Oval this afternoon.'

Nigey Havers, who was playing table tennis with Whiffy Day Lewis, made a pointed remark about it being nearly lunchtime and there wasn't a single ruddy foot of film in the can. But still 'Hiram F. Hamburger' was not ready, and with a moody shrug of his shoulders he retired to his caravan to brood.

Bomber Piggot-Smith, who of course has a marvellous throwing arm, lobbed a few stink-bombs through the vehicle's ventilator to try and flush him out, but still they waited. At last, Pranger Everett organized a de-bagging party and that finally seemed to knock some spirit into the reluctant waffle-nosher.

The fatal scene was shot and the American was quite marvellous. But he was no more marvellous than the others. They were all as marvellous as each other, which just goes to show.

The difference is that English actors (Hoedown-Hanks please note) are able to be marvellous without making quite such a song and dance about it.

I yield to no one in my admiration for the naturalistic style of some of these slack-jawed gum-chewers. Contemplating your navel and going mumble-wumble-bumble doesn't get you very far in a theatre, of course, but it can be brilliantly effective on celluloid, as I am the first to admit.

It has to be said though, that American acting does lack the gut-wrenching, primal thrillingness of English acting, and American actors know absolutely nothing about the classics and the wonderful productions which were done at Epidauros thousands of years ago. But, as anyone who has travelled across America (as I did with *Henry the Eighth*) will tell you, it is a very, very young country. It has no culture as such, except for the Red Indians who are marvellous, and they think you're absolutely mad if you walk anywhere.

But to stay with the Red Indians for a bit: I found that, sharing as we do a heritage stretching back to the mists of time, I had more in common with them than with any of the Klondike Charlies I met on my travels. Wandering about the reservations of Colorado, I sometimes felt that I had truly 'come home'. I shall never forget the beautiful starlit night when I was made an honorary brave of the Yankton Sioux. They gave me the tribal name of He Who Has A Great Organ For A Head, because of my trained voice I suppose. I shall probably return there one day to take my place as an elder of the tribe. I love Red Indians.

American character acting – now there is a curious phenomenon. It seems that John Malco-Twitch or someone has only to put on a false nose and have his head shaved for everyone to acclaim him as a Protean genius. And yet in England we have scores of actors who are able to transform themselves so completely that they are unrecognizable even to members of their own families. Anything less like an elephant than John Hurt would be hard to imagine, and yet by sheer concentration and use of his tool he became one. As for the persecuted homosexual he played in *Captain Corelli's Mandolin*, well, Hurty is very much a 'birds and pints' man, I can assure you. Again, Brian Blessed, bless him, has a massive screen presence but in reality he only weighs $9\frac{1}{4}$ stone, and has done since leaving the Police Force in 1963. Brian uses no padding, no cushions up his jumper, he merely has to *think* bulky and hey presto! Augustus Caesar – Prince Vultan.

Oh yes, the Americans are some way behind us yet I feel.

The Men with Cigars

'Mister Di Capri would like to meet with you,' said a marshmallow Manhattan voice down the telephone. Apparently I was supposed to be deeply impressed by this since

Lorenzo in *The Duke of Pisa* (Brazilian rain forest tour).

the said Mr Di Capri is some sort of movie mogul. Not being much of a cinema-goer, I had not heard of the gentleman. (Of course I absolutely love old films and I can recite the dialogue of every single Ealing comedy ever made at the drop of a hat, but I'm always far too busy (fortunately) to actually *go* to the cinema. I'll perhaps go to a concert occasionally, as I'm extraordinarily passionate about serious music, or if I'm tired I might stick a video in the machine, but for spiritual revival it's the theatre, the theatre and the theatre (in that order!). People say to me, 'Don't you get bored with it?' but my answer is always the same: 'Did Galileo get bored with the stars, did Leonardo get bored with thinking?')

It was hardly surprising I suppose that after my success with Truepate, and the award, I was to be 'checked out' by the corona-toting fraternity. And so it was that I found myself in Mr Di Capri's suite at the Dorchester, glass of Champoo in hand, being ushered in to see the great man. For someone who was supposed to be so desperate to meet me, he seemed to know remarkably little about my career. Of *The Dogs of Tblonsk* he had never heard, and I had serious doubts about whether he had ever seen *The Cuckolde of Leicester*. He surveyed me briefly through a cloud of cigar smoke before thanking me profusely for coming, then buzzing for a flunky to show me out. That was it. In the limousine home I found myself wondering what had happened to all this impeccable American courtesy we are always being told about.

A week later I found myself installed, at Mr Di Capri's behest, in a suite at the Beverly Wilshire Hotel. A succession of faceless suits arrived daily to drag me off to lunch or dinner at some fashionable eatery, which was all right except that they gave me so much in expenses that I lived in constant terror of being mugged. It was a nightmare.

By and large, I found Hollywood an extraordinary place. It has a strange atmosphere – a sort of 'weirdness'. And the people are quite remarkable in an odd kind of way, with a very unusual quality. All in all, I found the whole LA experience rather unreal.

After about ten days I was summarily informed that the film project was cancelled. I was paid off in a rather peremptory way and given a first-class ticket back to London.

Of course, not every brush with the film world throws up a horror story like this, but one really does wonder why so many smashing actors turn their backs on the theatre to go and work in such a tawdry medium. I think one of the saddest sights I ever saw was Michael Caine sauntering out of Maxim's in Paris and getting into a white Rolls-Royce.

'You silly, silly, silly, silly, *silly* man!' I thought. 'What *are* you doing? You could be playing Justice Shallow in The Pit. You could be working with Peter Gill's experimental group at the National – doing some *real* acting.' Funny things happen, don't they, when people start to believe their own publicity? I'm just very glad I've got my head screwed on sometimes.

Indian Adventure

But as I say, not all one's dealings with the film world are unpleasant. I had an absolute ball making the Mother Teresa movie. Smashing people and a script which had some enormously important things to say about the glorious heyday of the Raj, and about poverty of course, an issue which tends to make me very, *very* angry. And then there was the experience of India herself: vast, immense, a limitless landscape the sheer scale of which hardly anyone seems to appreciate, which always slightly astonishes me – however. As far as the subcontinent and I were concerned it was love at first sight and it is practically certain that I will go back there to live permanently one day, work permitting.

We were all one big happy family on *Teresa* and Meryl was quite brilliant as well as being almost an absolute dream to work with (poor sausage, she always has so much riding on her shoulders that she finds it very difficult to be just 'one of the cast', which is a shame but understandable). I was playing Fanshawe, one of the subalterns who fall passionately in love with the young Teresa at the Delhi Durbar of 1925. I had a couple of big scenes with Meryl and a few days of mess-room horseplay, but apart from that I was free to travel around discovering the *real* India: the subtle shades, the delicate aromas and the sheer enormousness of the place.

The film was an absolute feast for the eye. The heroic scale of Meryl's work among the sick and starving was superbly evoked. Anyone who remembers the ravishing spectacle of the big ballroom scene with Meryl and I and the others will probably be amazed to learn about an extraordinarily hair-raising episode which occurred the night before we shot the sequence.

Whenever I'm filming and I have an important scene to do the next day, I make it a hard and fast rule to be in Bedfordshire by six p.m. and pulling into Noddington Junction by seven at the latest. On this occasion I was snoozing away under the mosquito net when, at about ten-thirty, I was wrenched from the arms of Morpheus by the sound of splintering wood, followed by a loud crash as my bedroom door gave way. Peering into the gloom, I was just able to make out a familiar and slightly unsteady figure. It was none other than that notorious hell-raiser and public school hero of many a Raj epic, my old mate Ben McCorkindale. He was stark naked and had a smouldering firework on his head.

'Get your clothes off,' said Ben, 'we're going out.'

'Oh no, Ben. Not tonight,' I protested feebly.

How he manages to project this image of clean-cut innocence on a nightly regimen of carousing and roistering is a mystery to me. Smashing actor though, Ben. Some people say he was nothing before David Puttnam got hold of him and trained him up, but in fact he had done lots of good work before then at Sheffield, and he can play Rattigan like an angel, the bugger.

As we hopped starkers across the *maidan*, swigging at a bottle of brandy, I found myself wondering why it is that Ben always brings out the scamp in me. Some devil seems to enter my head when Ben looms into view bearing red paint and brushes. That night it seemed the most sensible thing in the world to uproot a jacaranda tree, load it on to a tonga, take it to the other side of Jaipur and plant it in a chilli field while singing the *Marseillaise*. Mad. Completely mad.

I was ready for my bed after that but no, said Ben, we had to celebrate our achievement in proper style. So we had a mud fight then headed off into town.

If you have ever tried to buy '66 Krug in Jaipur after midnight you will know what a hopeless task it is. They haven't really got anything much worth buying there, and why should they have? They are a developing nation with enormous problems. It always vaguely staggers me that some people go out to India expecting Harrods on every street corner. It's just a bit silly really.

Anyway, Ben and I fell to drinking in a hotel bar with a chap who told us that the nearest half-decent Champoo was in an off-licence in Kabul. I climbed on to the table and started to do the St. Crispin's Day speech from *Harry Five*. I was pretty soon up to full vol. with the diaphragm pumping like a beam engine, and by the time I got to 'Then will he strip his sleeve and show his scars,' Ben had persuaded the chap to fly us over the Afghan border in his private plane.

'We'll buy one bot, OK,' I said to Ben as we winged our way over the Hindu Kush, 'and then it's straight home to Bedfordshire.' But he had that impish twinkle in his eye which usually means that events are going to take a still more bizarre turn. Sure enough, after we touched down in Kabul he marched across to a Russian* armoured vehicle, bowed to the senior officer and announced, 'Mr Craig and I are celebrated English actors. We require a Jereboam and two fat women for our pleasure.' Which was fairly typical McCorkindale.

'Please let's go back to the hotel,' I pleaded, since it was very cold on the runway with no clothes on. The Russian fixed me with a cold cruel stare, barked an instruction to his subordinate and we were forced at gun-point into the back of the vehicle and driven off at high speed, joggle joggle. The comrades were impervious to my protestations about having to be in make-up

---

*The Taliban have since ousted the Russians from this part of the world, demonstrating that in freedom-fighting, as in film-making, 'less is more'. And while I'm still very much in two minds about fundamentalism, I don't believe it does anything like as much harm as American global capitalism with its Burger Kings and its bloody Sock Shops everywhere. The abandonment of spirituality in Western society makes about as much sense to me as trying to do without one's feet.

by seven-thirty. So there we were, jolting through the Afghan night, completely pissed and without the faintest idea where we were going.

We were given a heroes' reception back at the Russian military base, also a bottle of vodka and two badges which we later discovered were The Supreme Order of Bravery. To make matters worse, the Commanding Officer insisted that we fly back with him to his home town for a special celebration breakfast. There was no gainsaying him, and ninety minutes later we found ourselves tucking into Borscht, black bread and yet more vodka in his luxury abode in Omsk, and being gawped at the while by a group of assorted babushkas.

To my absolute horror, our host's mother recognized me from a sitcom I had been in some years before. *Oh No! It's the Neighbours* was apparently just as popular in its dubbed Russian form as it was in England. 'Oi nyet – eti sossyedi!' she cackled. Then she prodded me and sang the theme music. So there we were, Craig and McCorkindale at three a.m. in the middle of Siberia, absolutely paralytic and Harry Starkers to boot.

'How the bloody hell are we going to get back?' I asked Ben, 'we must be nearly two thousand miles from the hotel.'

'There's only one thing to do,' he said, as they cleared the room for dancing, 'telex O'Toole.'

'O'Toole?'

'He'll tell us what to do next. He's been on more hilarious madcap escapades than you and I have had hot dinners.'

It made sense of course, and I was rather touched by the enormous respect which Ben clearly had for his hero.

'PETER, HELP!' we tapped out frantically on the C.O.'s machine, 'WE'VE BEEN HELL-RAISING ALL NIGHT AND WE CAN'T GET BACK TO OUR HOTEL. PLEASE ADVISE. P.S. THOUGHT YOU WERE SMASHING IN LAWRENCE OF ARABIA.'

'BLESS YOU' came the reply, 'I'LL DO MY BEST BUT IT'S BEEN A GOOD FEW YEARS YOU KNOW. WHERE ARE YOU?'

'OMSK.'

'TRICKY. ARE YOU TOTALLY PISSED AND IN THE NUDE?'

'YES.'

'THAT'S SOMETHING THEN. I THINK YOU'LL HAVE TO RECITE ESKIMO NELL THEN RUN ABOUT PRETENDING TO BE MONKEYS. GOOD LUCK. LOVE PETER.'

Well – *it worked!!!*

At six-thirty a.m. we stepped unsteadily from a supersonic Soviet reconnaissance plane on to the tarmac at Jaipur. We had just enough time to replace the jacaranda, have a quick mud fight and get back to the hotel to dress before the cars came to take us to the location.

Hung over, jetlagged and with about a gallon of black coffee sloshing about inside us, we staggered on to the set. How we managed to get our lines out will always be a mystery to me, but you know what? It was the best scene in the film.

Mad about the thane. As Macbeth for Gay Sweatshop at the Drill Hall, 1989.

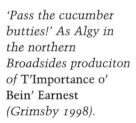

'Pass the cucumber butties!' As Algy in the northern Broadsides produciton of T'Importance o' Bein' Earnest *(Grimsby 1998).*

7

Acto Ergo Sum

Comedy

The first thing to be absolutely clear about as far as comedy is concerned is that it is a *desperately* serious business. Serious and tough. You have only to watch master comedians like Peter Bowles and Anton Rogers at work to realize there is nothing remotely amusing about it. It is far and away the most serious kind of acting there is, and if, even for one tiny fraction of a second, an actor in a comedy is *not* serious about it (i.e. funny) he is absolutely lost. He might as well go home, throw away his bullworker and burn his jazz pants. The comic actor must be as serious as a shark in southern waters, as real as the nose on his face, as honest as a simple shepherd boy at play on the Atlas mountains.

Martin Clunes confessed to me that he was funny once and the experience so shook him that he nearly gave up the profesh entirely, poor bunting.

So, in my book, Comedy = Seriousness + Toughness (and timing – very important. TIMING). Some people are born with it, some people acquire it and some people never get it. I have heard a whisper that Simon Williams managed to pick it up in Bangkok on a punishing Far Eastern tour.

There are a few basic rules of timing which any competent actor ought to be able to follow, like facing out front to deliver a punchline and giving a little cough at the end of it, or doing a false trip and blowing a raspberry as you exit, but these are just the tip of the timing iceberg. To be a really successful timer you need to have the accuracy of a chronometer and the instinct of a lynx. You need to have spotted boxer shorts, sock-suspenders and that little inner voice which tells you that precise moment to squirt yourself with a soda syphon and run about the stage going 'Oooooooh!' It is a rare and precious gift.

Timing cannot be taught. Although I am one of those infuriating people blessed with faultless timing, it would be impossible for another actor to copy me successfully. It is a personal thing. My timing is my timing is my timing. It is not *his* timing or *her* timing but *mine*. It is my watermark, my DNA chain, my footprint in the sands of European Drama. It is unpredictable, mysterious, soft and special – it is me.

Farce

If comedy is serious, farce is an absolutely tragic form. 'Oh, but farce is smashing fun,' I hear you demur. Well, yes of course, it is a tremendous giggle and one always adores doing it, but playing farce requires the precision of a Swiss laser surgeon cutting diamonds for his life while sitting on an unexploded bomb at the foot of Mount St Helen's. And the other thing about farce is that it is *such*, such hard work.

When I was in *Pardon my Privates* at the Garrick I nearly collapsed with exhaustion after every performance. At the time I was under the kind of pressure which would have sent many an accountant or so-called publisher scurrying to his bed wailing for cold compresses. But I went on and 'did it' because I had to, because I am a professional. Unlike a publisher, say, an actor cannot ring up the rest of the cast and say, 'Oh dear, would you mind saying all my lines as well as your own because I've got to go to the Frankfurt Book Fair,' or, as I was once told when I rang up a certain publisher's office: 'Sorry,

Farce – essentially a tragic form.

Lucinda's away for the weekend' (and this on a *Thursday*, mark you). It is at times like this that you suspect you're in the wrong business. However. Such is life.

Anyway, in I went to the Garrick, night after night, eight shows a week. (I wonder how many publishers could manage that – eight *lunches* a week, possibly.) On I went, up I cheered, out I bashed it, and about I made the audience fall with laughter, while my life in the daytime was in total chaos.

The reason for my low state was that I had made an offer on the Richmond house, only to have *three* buyers at the Clapham end drop out within two months of each other. It was a nightmare which looked like dragging on until the crack of doom.

But then Simon Charitymatch, bless him, brought an estate agent pal of his along to see *Privates*. Now what would have happened if I had been a split-second out with my timing that evening, I dread to think, but as it turned out I was spot on as usual and the estate agent absolutely adored the show. He immediately took up my problem and within a month – a little month – I was down at Laura Ashley's choosing wallpapers. But for my farce precision, I might still be living in Clapham (or even Islington, which I considered for a while). The thought makes me go cold because I have now become so utterly attached to Richmond that I couldn't imagine living anywhere else. People say it's a bit of a trek into town, but I can do some journeys quicker than when I was in Clapham. If I'm working at the Nash, I can leave Marchmont Road at, say, ten a.m. – eight-minute walk to the station – twelve minutes on the train – seven minutes along the walkway to the South Bank – pick up mail at the stage door, quick giggle with Frank – and by 10.29 I can be standing on the Lyttelton stage with a coffee ready to start rehearsals. So much for Richmond being 'a bit of a way out'. And as for the planes – well, after a week or so you just don't notice them.

Shakespeare

Asking me to write an objective analysis of Shakespeare is rather like asking Tristan to make a list of Isolde's bad points or Mozart to say whether he thinks there's any point in music. Shakespeare is my first and last love, my *raison d'acter*, my Gioconda, my lost city of Atlantis. I love him.

> *Shakespeare:* Oh for God's sake, Nick, let's have a bit more hard info and a bit less purple prose.
> *Ego:* Sorry, Will, but you know how I feel about your writing. Ever since you came to live in the pit of my stomach I've found it very hard to be objective about you. Besides, interpretation is such a personal thing. What's right for me may not be right for another actor.
> *Shakespeare:* Enough of this intellectualizing, I'm off to the tavern for some ale and wenches. Coming, Nick?
> *Ego:* I'll join you later. Mine's a pint if you're getting them in.

One of the best pieces of advice I've ever had about playing Shakespeare was given to me by that deceptively absent-minded genius, John Barton. He looked at me one morning in rehearsals and said, 'I've just finished my egg hello is Gower playing? Cuckoo-cuckoo-cuckoo diaphragm weeeeeeee Hitler has only got one ball . . .' I tried to get him to be more specific but he went off to wrestle with a prolapsed iamb before he could elaborate. What I think he was saying is this: an actor playing Shakespeare must be an active volcano ready to erupt at any moment showering the audience with molten lava, he must also be a bee who can sting them and then cover them with honey, but before he can be either of these things he must be an acorn who doesn't come to rehearsals armed with a lot of preconceived ideas about the play.

Let us look at a well-known piece of Shakespeare: the chorus's opening speech from *Henry V:*

O for a muse of fire, that would ascend
The brightest heaven of invention!
A kingdom for a stage, princes to act
And monarchs to behold the swelling scene.

What exactly is Will saying to us in these four lines? What are the chorus telling us about themselves? Are we to attach any significance to the author's uncharacteristic omission of the word 'coxcomb'? Let us look at the section a little more closely to see if we can find the answers.

O *(The Globe Theatre)* for a muse of fire, *(The chorus want to burn the theatre down)* that would *(Would = fire-wood. Again the fire image)* ascend

The brightest heaven of invention! *(The smoke from the fire would have gone straight up into the sky because the Globe had no roof. It is fairly clear that the chorus are in combative mood, smarting no doubt from some high-handed act on the part of the management.)*

A kingdom for a stage, *(A favourite exclamation of Shakespeare's, c.f. 'My kingdom for a horse!')*

Princes to act *(The chorus want to play princes, they are fed up with carrying spears.)*

And monarchs to behold the swelling scene. *(Monarch's was probably a Tudor casting agency.)*

Now it is possible that one or two of these points will be missed by the audience. No matter, it is Will's way of telling actors where they are coming from, where they are going and what they had for breakfast. Will invariably tells you how to do it; he tells you when to crouch, when to shout, when to jump off a rostrum, when to put your hands on your hips and go

'Ha!'; he tells you to go fast where the jokes are in Latin, he tells you to be louder when the girl is wearing a transparent costume. In short, Will is your director.

I have found that having him living in a little thatched cottage in my stomach means that I hardly have to think about how to play him at all. I just open my mouth and it happens, out it all comes. I am the medium through which he speaks to the world, I am his woofer and his tweeter, his volcano, his bee, his combine harvester, his bondsman, his Sancho Panza, his Pele, his Master of Ballantrae –

Shakespeare: Nick, you daft old bugger, come and have a pint. You're as bad as Burbage. Congratulations on the award by the way . . .

Sybil Thorndike, a self-con-fessed 'cricket nut', keeps tabs on events at Trent Bridge during a matinee of Henry IV, part 1 *(1945).*

Alan Howard – 'A larynx like leather, able to do three big kings in a week,' as Terry Hands observed.

Political Theatre

People often say to me, 'Come on, Nick, are you a Marxist? Are you a Socialist? Or are you an SLDPXY – bloody – Z man?' But my answer always has to be the same – 'Christ! I don't know! I am an actor.' – it is the answer I have to give to a great many questions I am asked. The trouble is that I am so many things: I am me, I am you, I am Lord Foppishness. I am a nineteenth-century French balloonist, I am a mole and I live in a hole for Christ's sake, but *I am an actor*.

This is not to say that politics is not important to me, it is important – very important – but the actor part of me must remain above party wranglings. Now Equity, of course, by its very nature has to be a trade union, and Vanessa is a dear girl and a bloody good actress, but she's mad, quite, quite mad. What has the WRP got to do with the theatre? What's it got to do with bums on seats? No. I'm sorry Vanessa, I love you and your Masha was sublime but your politics are out to lunch.

Talking of which, Timmy Piggot-Smith has just given me a mind-blowing recipe: Ronald Merrick Marsala: Basmati rice; turmeric; half a chicken; loads of Indian spices. Try it.

But I digress. It seems to me that the whole notion of political debate in the theatre has become polarized. The polarity is such that we have, on the one hand, a political (per se) debate and on the other hand a more broadly based debate, and between the two we have this tremendous, as I say, polarity. Nobody is debating the important issue, which is the kind of debate we should be having. Everyone's too busy rushing to the Left or the Right or into the Middle Ground. Still, I'm basically optimistic for the future.

In the Seventies I was very active in political theatre. I have moderated my views somewhat since then but I am still immensely proud of the work I did with companies like *Shared Dressing Room* and *19:74*. (The Seventies was very much my

Pryce in boots.

period. It was an enormously exciting time. We had platform shoes, *The Onedin Line*, McKellen at his best and there was this tremendous sense of being slap bang between the Sixties and the Eighties). 19:74 was committed to producing politically-based work moving towards looser structures and a major reappraisal of the events leading up to the closure of the Smethwick arm of the Grand Union Canal in 1872. Yes, I know we were trying to achieve the impossible and yes, I know you can't create a new society overnight but at least we were trying. And I think the fact that we were never asked to return to any of the community centres in the Smethwick area shows that we were presenting our case rather too convincingly for certain people.

So if you're thinking of going into political theatre, be prepared for a lot of hard work and crossness. If you can bear eating McDonald's twice a day and the long company meetings about washing up, then political theatre is a great life.

Ensemble Playing and Improvisational Techniques

'Eating bacon is a political act.' – Snoo Wilson
'Theatre is a salad.' – Peter Brook

These were the founding principles of *Meaningful Experience*, the brilliantly innovative company with whom I spent a very happy couple of years in the early Seventies. The idea was that if an actor was freed from the constraints of costumes and dialogue, he would be able to transform himself from a wealthy merchant into a hard-pressed peasant within the blink of an eye, and without anyone having to sing a song about harvesting to give him time to change.

Meaningful Experience was started by the prodigiously talented Mike Michaels, a larger than life figure whose unconventional directing methods hit the theatrical establishment of the East Midlands like a tidal wave. He taught me more about nudity in relation to the industrial architecture of Coventry than almost any other man.

Ensemble acting is based on mutual trust between actors. Apart from a bean-bag and a copy of *Das Kapital*, the most important thing an ensemble actor must bring to a rehearsal is trust. For how can actors form a human pyramid together or convincingly portray a large piece of factory machinery if they do not trust their fellows? It is hard sometimes for us to trust each other from Day One of rehearsals, so we must use special warm-up exercises to speed up the familiarizing process. *At The Lunatic Asylum* is a good ice-breaker, also *Last Day at Nursery School*. But number one in my book has always been *Breakfast Time in the Chimp House*.

There are some people who are temperamentally suited to ensemble work and some who aren't. Despite my anarchic temperament, my outspokenness and my tireless championing of causes like the rain forests, the poor and the preservation of those delightful old 'K2' telephone boxes, I am passionately interested in other people. Other men and women are what fascinate me – my fellow human beings. I am very much a team man and *Meaningful Experience* was an ideal seed-bed for my talent to flourish in.

I remember when Mike called us together on that first cold morning. 'We have no script,' he said, 'no scenery, no costumes and no bookings. This mix has *got* to work.' Well, I think it did in the end but, dear God, it wasn't easy.

When Mike announced that we were going to adapt Proust's *A la Recherche du Temps Perdu* to our unique performance style, we were all stunned. Those in the cast who had read the books could recall no references to the Tolpuddle Martyrs, Grimaldi or the Three Day Week and we shuddered to think what audiences would make of it.

It took us a week to get used to each other's nudity and a further eight months to read all fifteen vols of *The 'Cherche* (although, for my part, I deliberately watched TV or went out in the evenings so as not to form too rigid a view of the work, to keep my canvas blank).

Mike was very tough with us in rehearsals but I thrive on slog and I found the experience exhilarating. Using nothing but our naked bodies, we managed to recreate in minute detail the *fin de siècle* world in which Proust's masterwork is set; one minute one was playing a chaise longue, the next a glass of absinthe, and all the time the great sweep of Proust's narrative was galloping past.

The first dress rehearsal of the show took eleven weeks, which was absurdly long, but after a hard night's cutting and trimming we managed to get the running time down to a more manageable two months. Many of us still thought this was too long for a show with no music or scenery, and we gloomily predicted that within ten days of the curtain going up we would hear the tell-tale sounds of coughing and fidgeting which warn you that you are 'losing' an audience. Mike was blithely confident, however, and assured us that *The 'Cherche* was *formidable.*

The first performance was remarkable. For a start we all mimed our good luck prezzies and cards and had such huge giggles trying to guess what we had given each other that we were two minutes late in starting. The audience responded to the production immediately though, and the only restlessness we detected was during a spell of particularly warm weather in the second half of August, and as the days got shorter and one began to feel that distinct nip in the morning air, the audience's concentration intensified.

Big hugs in the bar afterwards, and oh what bliss to get back into one's clothes again.

'Swannderful!' proclaimed the *Observer*. We were a hit. The tragedy was that so many people were unable to see the play from start to finish. One great heart took a year's sabbatical and saw all six performances, but on the whole houses were disappointingly thin.

Ensemble work can be enormously rewarding, but it is hard and reviewers *do* tend to get muddled about who played what, and one can find one's own performance being credited to someone who was quite frightful. Still, it's swings and roundabouts, I suppose.

Television

BBC Commissionaire: Yes, young man.

Ego: My name is Nicholas Craig and I have come to record a play.

BBC Commissionaire: Got a pass, have you?

Ego: I am an actor. Television plays cannot be recorded without actors. (POLITELY) Please let me through.

BBC Commissionaire: I'll see if you're on the list. What's your name again?

Sadly, this is a true story, and what is more, it happened only a week after I had won my award for Best Actor In A Hitherto Unperformed Late Jacobean Tragedy. Coming from the theatre, where everyone is generally a love, it is a terrible shock to come up against the bureaucracy of a large TV company. And as for all those secretaries and admin personnel scurrying about, well, what do they *do*? There are more technicians alone at the BBC than there are actors. It is frightening. I wonder how many people switch on the telly to watch Viv the vision-mixer or Wendy the wages clerk or Peter the programme planner? Not very many, I suspect. No, what Mr and Mrs Joe Public want to watch when they come home after a hard day at the factory is actors – *acting*. As soon as the men in charge wake up to this simple fact and leaven their mind-numbing output of documentaries and sport with a few more plays then – *then* – you will see viewing figures soar. Mark my words.

It's such a shame and so silly when the standard of television used to be so much higher. I remember when I first came into the profession as a nipper there used to be plays on TV nearly every night. Plays about real people, real characters who did real things like have affairs with Billie Whitelaw or go home to visit their working-class parents and cause trouble. Nowadays, what do we get? Snooker. Snooker and darts and women talking about their insides.

One of my first jobs as a fledgling actor was in a live television play. Now perhaps I should explain to my younger readers that television in those days was *not* recorded, it was done totally live, absolutely like a stage performance, except in front of a camera instead of an audience. It was absolutely terrifying of course, but great fun. If anyone died or the studio burnt down it was no good yelling 'cut', you bloody well had to keep going. It was all live in those days, you see.

This yellowing *Radio Times* cutting is in pride of place on page one of my scrapbook:

9.25

SUNDAY NIGHT THEATRE

presents

Drizzle at the Bus Queue

by Stanley Norman.
Billy is a bit of a dreamer, his mates at the factory trip him up and laugh at him, Mr Fazakerley says 'Now then' and lots of girls get pregnant.

Cast in order of appearance
Billy .... H.B. MALTRAVERS
Sam .... RICHARD BRIARS
Ted (The Foreman) ....
BARRINGTON   WETHERALL-GORE
Mr Fazakerley .... REX KING
Valerie .... CELIA WINSTANLEY
Doreen .... VIRGINIA MCKENNA
Factory Lads ...... NICHOLAS CRAIG,
EDWARD FOX, GARETH HUNT,
MICHAEL YORK.

Directed by Brian Curacao
Produced by Hugh Raconteur DFC

H.B. Maltravers and Rex King are appearing in 'ON DECK!' at the Prince of Wales Theatre.

Great days. But we mustn't get too depressed, I have done some smashing things on the box – and hope to do many more. Also, and I hope this doesn't sound arrogant, I happen to know that I'm bloody good at it. I learned very quickly that the secret of telly is to keep everything very small. Everything has to come right down: voice, gestures, make-up, even underpants if it's a Dennis Potter.

Television is about doing nothing. And nothing, but nothing, is harder than nothing.

And the recognition it brings you is quite astounding. I don't think it's any exaggeration to say that after the first series of *Oh No! It's the Neighbours* my face was as well-known as any member of the Royal Family's. If I happened to be walking around a shopping centre in the Midlands the day after a transmission, I would be literally mobbed. It's hardly surprising when one analyses it, because when you appear in someone's living room once a week, you become part of their lives – their property, in a sense. I'm not sure, though, that that accounts for some of the totally priceless things people say to you in the street.

Totally Priceless Things People Say to You in the Street

'You look so much older in real life.' (Thank you!)

'Eeee, I thought you was lovely last night. My sister says you were on her telly an' all.' (!)

'Our cat goes straight off to sleep when you're on.' (Charming!)

Sometimes I find the pressure too much:

> *Gushing Lady*: You must be tremendously brave to be an actor.

> *Craig:* As you must be, Madam, to wear that hat.

(Wicked, but I couldn't resist it. But all these slights and unintended insults are cancelled out by a letter like this:)

34 Talybont Mansions
Talybont Road
Cardiff

Dear Mr Craig,
I knew the first time what I saw you that I was watching an immense talent. It seems incredible to me that you is acting with even more charismatic intensity than then. What I did find tremendously exciting is the way what you make Jeremy Irons, Charles Dance and Anthony Andrews look like complete amateurs. They must hate you, wot with that and the award.

Love,
Nicola Llewellyn

I hasten to point out that I am of course Jerry, Charlie and Tone's greatest fan, as they are mine, but it's a sweet letter, isn't it? And one of thousands like it.

It was odd, after having established oneself very near the top of the theatrical tree, suddenly to be recognized for being in a TV show.

Oh No! It's The Neighbours, by the way, was the brainchild of a clever young writer just down from Manchester University whose name I never could remember. We used the normal domestic setting but it was a very long way indeed from being a run-of-the-mill situation comedy. We had to fight long and hard with the powers that be to get it put on.

'You're pushing the boundaries of television just too far,' they said.

'Good,' we said. 'We don't want to do just another sit-com.'

Our idea was revolutionary, certainly. It was this: both the mother *AND* the father of the household went out to work. There could be no scenes in the daytime, obviously. Everything had to take place at breakfast or in the evening. It was white knuckle time at the first recording, I can tell you. But it worked a treat of course. Since then there have been several unsuccessful attempts to copy our unique 'I'm home, Darling – So am I, Darling' format.

I played the punk son, Gob. It was a lovely part and the extensive research I did in Brixton certainly paid off. Great people, punks, and not at all what you'd expect. One I met was very interested in becoming an actor. I love punks.

The Power of Television

After one series of *Oh No! It's The Neighbours.*

> *BBC Commissionaire:* Morning Mr Gob. Park wherever you want.
> *Ego:* My name is Nicholas Craig and I am an actor. Gob is the name of the part I play.
> *BBC Commissionaire:* Sorry Sir, just my way.

Commercials

Are lovely.

I suppose I am destined to be associated with a certain brand of specially mild coffee for the rest of my days. But if you ask me if it is irritating to have people shouting 'Extra Mild Blend' when they see me in the street, I would say 'No' without hesitation. Look, the time to start worrying about recognition is when it stops. And I am always ever so slightly dumbfounded when other actors ask me, 'How can you do commercials, Nick? You're a serious classical actor.' Am I being cynical, or is it only those who don't get offered advertising work who ask these questions?

To me, there is no conflict between advertising and straight acting: one is wearing a costume, one is in front of a camera and one is speaking. What's the big difference? And in all three of the commercials we have made so far, we have always tried to tell a truthful human story; first there was the rain-ruined barbecue, then the shelves which fell down as soon as I looked the other way, and, lastly, the one in which I get bowled out first ball – all little plays, if you like, and all requiring just as much skill as anything by Ibsen or Shakespeare. And, in any case, I haven't made nearly as much out of them as people think.

Radio

I am one of those people who would quite happily live on a spike in the middle of the Sahara desert as long as I could listen to Radio 4. I love radio. It always mildly astonishes me that some people seem to regard radio as a poor relation. Not in my book, it isn't. And of course it's the most civilized medium of all to work in.

Charles Dance, Robert Powell, Jeremy Irons and Anthony Andrews have all proved themselves to be first-rate broadcasters, and the great thing about radio is that a lack of physical beauty is no handicap.

What a super old building Broadcasting House is. Retaining, as it does, many delightful 1930s period features and administrative staff, it is a feast of art deco. And how proudly dear old 'B.H.' bears her battle scars. There is still a hole in the wall of the contracts office from that terrible night in December 1940 when Uncle Mac lost his temper over some late rehearsal payments.

I don't think it is generally known that two hundred feet below Portland Place there is a fully operational studio equipped with enough scripts and actors to continue broadcasting *Afternoon Theatre* for up to fifteen years after a nuclear strike.

Broadcasting House is also the home of the BBC Radio Drama Company; a highly skilled group of artists who have perfected the remarkable ability to produce, at a moment's notice, the authentic background sounds of anything from a thirteenth-century tavern to a First World War battle. To see one of these stalwart actors, with his crossword in his hand, marching on the spot in a tray of gravel and whistling 'Pack Up Your Troubles' is to witness true dedication to the craft of acting.

I absolutely love radio. In fact, if TV, films, the theatre, commercials, chat shows and industrial training films were to be abolished tomorrow, no one would be happier than I because it would mean that I could spend every single day and night of the rest of my life doing nothing but lovely radio. And of course one can do it on a Sunday, which would be absolutely ideal for me.

*A break in rehearsals with award-winning director Peter James.
Peter looks tired because he knows I'm right.*

8

All About Me

I have deliberately avoided writing about myself so far in this book. To be quite honest, I find it rather embarrassing. Not because of anything I may or may not have done while I was in *Mother Goose* at Portsmouth (and for which, in any case, I have paid my debt), but because I am basically a shy man. Now I know most people will be surprised to read that, but it's true. Self-analysis does not come easily to me.

I'll have a try, though.

I suppose the most remarkable thing about me is that although I'm a complete anarchist who totally rejects rules and regulations, although I can carry a packed theatre to the plains of Siberia and back with the flare of my nostril, and although I must seem like a god to some people, I am really a very ordinary sort of sausage-and-mash type of bloke. Just like everyone else, I get up, get drunk, go to the launderette, fall in love. What's godlike about that? No, I'm Mr Normal, I'm afraid. I lose my temper, I run out of milk. And you know those days when you lie in bed till the evening singing 'Fly Me to the Moon' in different accents and flicking bits of chewed up paper with an elastic band? Well, I have them too.

Ego: Hang on a second, d'you think this is wise
   Shouldn't the actor remain elusive? Mysterious?
Craig: Up to a point, but I've never been tremendously
   good at not being un-phoney with people.
Ego: All right. Carry on then.

Caught having a sinful Kit Kat.

Even though I have pursued success and perfection with the single-mindedness of a hungry barracuda who was always patronized by his elder brothers, I have always had a very, *very* wide range of other lifelong passions. Philosophy, early music, fine wine, theoretical physics, landscape gardening, medicine, cooking, anthropology and my collection of Victorian chamber-pots are all things which give me enormous satisfaction and help me to recharge my acting batteries. And then there are my friends. I have hundreds of friends outside the profession – historians, barristers, surgeons – with whom I have some tremendously interesting conversations, but a lot of the time they bore me and I find my mind wandering back to the rehearsal room and to my family, my real family, that is – the Theatre.

I act because I have to, because it's what I do best, and I suppose if I'm honest, because it's a way of avoiding real life.

You see, the problem that many actors have is that they don't know who they are. I have often looked at my award, with my name inscribed upon it, and asked out loud: 'Yes, but who *is* Nicholas Craig?' I know a lot of other actors have asked themselves the same question. People simply don't realize how immensely difficult it is for an actor to say, 'Don't worry, *I'll* do the shopping/clean the grill-pan/drive you to the hospital,' when he doesn't know who he is. It's all very well for you to say, 'Nicholas Craig is a successful actor/writer who lives in Richmond and is a bit of a maverick,' but I can't always see it as clearly as that.

As a vagabond barometer of the human condition it is all too easy to lose track of one's identity. I have a wonderful self-awareness exercise which I can recommend to any other actors who suffer as I do. What I do is this. Sit naked in front of a mirror and tell myself my life story. I usually have a big pile of old school reports and reviews beside me so that I can interrupt myself if I get details wrong. It's a trick Mike Michaels taught me when I was with *Meaningful Experience*. I've used it regularly ever since. I honestly think that if I didn't have my twice-weekly session I would start to lose touch with reality. As it is, I have managed to remain very down to earth as a person. Mind you, I always knew I was special, my mother drummed that into me at a very early age.

My Bedfordshire Book of Little Things

For many years now I have been jotting down my random thoughts and impressions concerning this old globe of ours and the hopeless creatures who dwell hereon. I call it my Bedfordshire Book because I write it last thing before climbing aboard the Noddington Junction special. It will probably be published in full one day (though not by the present publishers, of that you may be absolutely certain), but in the meantime here are a few snatches.

Just my Luck! (Extra Mild Blend coffee commercial, 1988.)

Little things which irritate one:

A passion flower that opens up the day after your al fresco luncheon party.

Playwrights who seem to think that one's only function is to say their lines.

Favourite little things:

Bill Wackerbath's speech impediment.

Apologies.

The recording of Elizabeth Schwarzkopf and Victoria de Los Angeles singing the cat duet.

Little things that dismay one somewhat:

People who don't appear to have done any rep.

Warm Beaujolais.

The threat of nuclear war.

Absolutely hateful things:

Second-rate olives.

The glaze on repro Staffordshire.

The way the press always manage to make one appear stupid and pretentious.

Things which are really rather saddening:

Someone who throws their stifado at you and calls you selfish even though it's you who has paid for the whole holiday.

Rain dripping from a sycamore leaf in the third week in August, then trickling on to a dahlia, staying there for a bit until a cat or something knocks it so that it dribbles down into the earth and is gone.

Deliciously illicit little things:

A mirror in the garden.

Ripping your copy of Interiors out of its polythene wrapper and going back to bed with it.

Being unfaithful to someone between shows on Saturday.

A damson in November.

Surprising little things:

Charles Dance played a badger at Swindon in 1971.

The sheer number of people who seem to think that acting is *easy*, for God's sake.

People who don't understand that one cannot be tied to one person.

Things which are so heavenly and life-affirming that they make you want to cry out, 'Yes! Yes!':

Lesbos after all the Italians have gone.

A well-restored cornice moulding.

Little things one wishes one could do without:

Russian tea sipped by an apple-wood fire on a drizzly afternoon six miles outside Bury St Edmunds.

Clingwrap.

Things one couldn't do without under any circumstances I'm afraid:

Fresh gooseberries.

My special stationery which I have made in Edinburgh.

Tears.

Victorian chamber-pots.

Lovingness.

Things which are brilliantly funny:

The cat duet again.

That piece of old film that shows Little Tich dancing in big shoes.

Things without which one would be perfectly content to do:

Frozen courgettes.

The press, although I know they've got a job to do.

People who never return their front door keys.

Things which seem to be appallingly complex then take on an autumnal wryness and finally turn out to be quintessentially feisty:

Terence Stamp.

Literary Me

Writing this book has certainly helped me to explore and reveal myself more thoroughly, and yet when I re-read what I have written, I feel as though I am looking at a Rembrandt sketch. It is intricate, it is honest, but it is incomplete. It is a portrait of an immediate man, a 'come on, let's get on with it' sort of chap. My prose conveys nothing of the quiet, reflective, rather bookish person who is perhaps the most real of all the me's.

I'm an academic at heart, and it is practically certain that one day I will end up as a fellow of some sleepy Oxford college, pottering across the quad in a pair of highly polished old brogues, long-waisted green cords, Harris tweed jacket in lovat with leather buttons, a knitted oatmeal tie with perhaps a Fairisle pullover and over it all a rather shabby, long black gown.

For summer wear I would have a pair of old grey flannels (or khaki drills), a loose-fitting cream silk shirt, MCC tie and

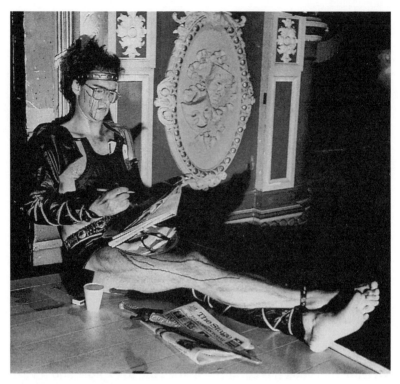

'Doing the crossword'.

alpaca jacket. My panama would be from Lock's and would have a ribbon in the colours of whichever college had awarded me my fellowship.

I think I would fit very well into the groves of academe because as well as being immensely passionate about books and literary criticism I would also be able to set whole faculties on a roar at dinner with my theatrical anecdotes.

Research has been an abiding passion of mine for as long as I can remember – all my characters are meticulously researched down to the last dab of nose-putty – and I have recently become completely hooked on literary sleuthing. Nothing gives me greater pleasure than to sit in a library examining texts and manuscripts for solutions to some of the great literary conundrums of our age, such as why did Wilfred Owen's creative juices dry up after 1918? What was wrong with E.E. Cummings's shift key? What does *Lord of the Flies* mean? Why on earth didn't Kenneth Branagh's smashing autobiography, *Branagh*, sell a bit better?

It was inevitable that before long my epistolary ratiocinations would throw up a subject which cried out to be staged.

Sure enough, I happened to have popped into W.H. Smith's one morning and, having a bit of time to kill, I began to browse through the books. My eye fell on a paperback edition of – well, you've guessed it – the correspondence between Sir Walter Scott and his publisher, Mr MacTavish.

By the time I got home to Richmond I had read the first ten pages and was enchanted. There was something about the intimacy of the letters, their inconsequentiality, which leapt off the page and pulled the reader back to the Selkirkshire of the early 1800s. It evoked the period and conjured up a whole social order in a way that dry old biographies never can do. Just little exchanges like this:

Dear Sir Walter,
Many thanks for your wee letter and invitation to tea on the 17th. We would verra much like to come. But unfortunately we can't.

Yours,
MacTavish.

P.S. Dinna trouble to write any more books just now as we have plenty of yours to be going on with.

My dear MacTavish,
Sorry you canna make the 17th. What about the 18th? It's nae trouble to write books. I enjoy it.

Yours,
Sir Walter.

P.S. I enclose some more Waverley novels.

I knew that I would not be able to sleep peacefully until I had put this relationship on a stage. That night I had to go in to the Nash to do a *Pisa* and, yes, I know it was unprofessional, but all through the perf I could think of nothing but the letters.

Over the next few weeks I began to appreciate the sheer scale of the task I was proposing to undertake. How could it be staged? How would one convey Scott's literary circle and the enormousness of the highland landscape? Who would play MacTavish and who would play his assistant, Hypatia? Was anyone really interested in the hot-house world of Scottish letters at the start of the 19th century? The problems seemed insoluble, and as the run of *The Duke of Pisa* came to an end I became profoundly bored with the whole project and abandoned it. I thought it would be much more fun instead to work on an idea that Simon Charitymatch and I had dreamed up, viz. – to take a sideways look at the grand old game of cricket in prose and poetry, with the occasional surprise.

Then an extraordinary thing happened.

I had arranged with Harriet Rackstraw to go down to her cottage near Chichester for a week to unwind and generally recharge the acting batteries after my punishing season at the Nash. On the train down there were two Scotsmen sitting nearby, which would have been nothing in itself, but when I got to Hat's cot, what should I see on the dining-room wall but a framed mezzotint of Landseer's 'Monarch of the Glen'. Everything was drawing my thoughts back to Sir Walter Scott and his world. I dug out my copy of the letters and, as I began to re-read, my pulse quickened and my acting Geiger counter went soaring into the red. There it all was again – the intimacy, the social history and of course the mouth-watering piquancy of Sir Walter's prose.

I think it was on the Tuesday morning, while I was walking to Worthing for breakfast, that I found myself reciting an

'*An outrageous thought struck me. Why shouldn't I play Sir Walter and Mr MacTavish?*'

exchange which had stuck in my mind from the previous night:

Dear Sir Walter,
We really canna publish any more o' this stuff o' yours.
It's incrrredibla boring and naebody will buy it.

– to which Walter movingly replies:

My dear MacTavish,
Och, please gie me one more chance. I've a canny plot
aboot a laddie name of Ivanhoe which I'm sure will make
a braw Xmas seller.

I was declaiming this across the South Downs when an outrageous thought struck me. Why shouldn't *I* play Sir Walter *and* Mr MacTavish?

Do the whole thing myself in casual evening dress and no scenery, and take it to theatres and community centres up and down the country for 250 notes a night and no questions asked?

Back in London, I set about research proper. I looked at every picture of Scotland I could lay my hands on, and read right to the end of the letters – a monumental task. I watched *Taggart*, I listened to James Naughtie and I started having porridge for breakfast every morning.

But how to reduce the enormous volume of correspondence to a manageable length? Which elements of the story could be dispensed with and which retained? Well, most of the fishing reports could go, certainly – and yet they had a captivating period charm. There was definitely no room for the plans of the new wing Walter was having built to accommodate his wife's family – but the contractor's estimates and the intricacies of the planning laws as they stood in 1801 were so freshly evoked that one could almost smell the newly painted guttering as one read. And really, it would be a crime to lose those tailor's bills.

No, the letters were uncuttable. It would have to be a six-hour show.

For the next year Walter never left my thoughts for more than a few seconds. I did other plays, played other parts, but my mind was geared up for one thing and one thing only – the first performance in the foyer of the National Theatre of *My Dear MacTavish*.

Would the audience stick with it? Would they get bored? Would they follow the heartless way MacTavish always fobbed Walter off with his assistant, Hypatia, and how Hypatia herself was often unable to deal with Walter's letters because she was either at the Highland Games or ill or at the Fraserburgh Book Fair? Would people be as captivated as I had been when I first discovered this epic human story? Looking back after four

'For six white-hot performance hours, these are my costumes, my scenery, my special effects'.

successful years of touring *My Dear MacTavish* around the country, those misgivings seem foolish. But the fact is that I didn't know whether I had pulled it off until the very end of that first performance, when I read out Walter's last defiant epistle:

My dear MacTavish,
All right then, how about if I were tae purchase your wee publishing company and pay your wages (nae more nor less than ye deserve, mind) and take over all your ootstanding debts? Well, ye'd be bound to put me between hard covers then, wouldn't ye? Or it'd be the puir hoos and nae breeches nor puddin' for thee. What have ye to say tae that, Mr Expensive Lunch and Half Moon Specs MacTavish?

The audience, however, were wonderful. Some of them coming out of shows in the Olivier and the Lyttelton were immediately won over and roared their approval.

Every time I give a performance of *My Dear MacTavish*, I discover something new in the wonderful writing and the humanity of the story. I haven't come near to getting it right yet and I don't suppose I ever will (an opinion which, in all fairness to myself, I should say is not shared by the majority of people who have seen *'Tavish*).

As for more one-man shows? Well, Simon Charitymatch has a scheme to perform all 135 editions of *Wisden*. Intriguing, but I worry about fitting Dennis Lillee's run-up into a small venue. Still, Hat's cot in Chich is available in Aug . . .

9

To the Young Actor

If a youngster comes to me and says, 'Mr Craig, I want to be an actor,' I tell him to go and boil his head. Only a complete and utter lunatic becomes an actor.

If the youngster insists, 'But, Mr Craig, I really do want to be an actor,' I clip him round the ear, kick him and tell him to go and do his A-levels.

If the obstinate young shaver sets his jaw, stamps his feet and shrieks, loud enough to wake the whole street up, 'Mr Craig, I mean to act!' it is at that point that I begin to take some notice of him. I turn to him, take a long cool look at him and then I ask him these eight basic questions: are you prepared to sweat and slog and suffer and slave? Are you ready to starve for very little money? Are you prepared to work so hard in your movement classes that your feet come off? Are you willing to work in the North of England? Do you have the dedication to spend your dole on silly little presents for people at the BBC who might possibly employ you? Do you have the sensitivity to sympathize with your agent's interior decor problems? Do flattery and apologizing come easily to you? And, above all, will you be able to learn the language of the profession and say things like 'Onwards and upwards', 'Oh well, we survive' and 'Never stops, love, he *never stops*'?

If he answers all these questions in the affirmative, I tell him to go away and work in an office for five years and then, *then*, if he still wants to act he should join an amateur theatre company as an assistant stage manager and there undertake the most menial and humiliating tasks he can find. If, when he has done all these things, he is still intent on making a career in the theatre then – well, I suppose he might as well go to drama school or he could try getting a job with a children's theatre company, it doesn't really make much difference, but it's no good him asking me for help because you're on your own in this business. It's tough with a capital 'T'. Look at Bette Davis, she suffered, but she survived. And even when she was breaking up inside, she could still go out there and wipe the floor with Lombard and Bacall and Stanwyck and all the others. And they knew it. That was why they tried to destroy her but they couldn't. She was just too great a star.

So, my young friend, if you are determined to take your chance on the boards, then be assured you will know poverty, pain, despair, illness, you may even die, but you will have chosen the greatest profession in the world; a way of life that will take you to the stars and back and make you a king, an emperor, a goddess, a vicar, a pirate, a nosey neighbour, a 2nd interfering bystander – anything. Whatever glittering prize or foaming chalice of ambrosia you want is yours for the taking.

Choosing a Drama School

Drama schools go in and out of fashion very quickly; some years LAMDA is the place to show your promise, other years the agents and casting directors will be beating a path down to Webber Douglas to pick up talent. It is impossible to say which schools will be 'in' two years hence.

Do not be seduced by glossy prospectuses. You only need to know two basic facts: how many prizes and medals are handed out at the end of the final year (you will want to have some sort of award to put on your CV when you leave), and how often are the study trips to the zoo (imitating animal behaviour is of course the most important skill for a young actor to acquire).

Holding on to the furniture – a common beginner's fault.

RADA has a splendid selection of awards for the final-year students, but the Central School is within walking distance of Regent's Park. Rose Bruford and The Poor School are probably too far away from any zoos to merit a place in the first division of drama schools.

While alumni of the Birmingham School of Speech Training and Dramatic Art loyally defend the virtues of the aviary in the botanical gardens at Edgbaston, a better all-round bet is the Bristol Old Vic Theatre School – a goodly clutch of awards, and practically next door to Johnny Morris's old stamping ground.

For me though, the King of Drama Schools is my old alma mater, Biddy Lanzarote's Academy of Dance and Dramatic Art. I had an absolute ball at BLADDA; not only was it handy for Whipsnade but, being the only male student, I had the pick of all the best heroic roles (I had a fair breadth of choice in matters amorous, too, but perhaps this isn't the time or place).

Choosing a Name

One of your first tasks on leaving drama school will be to choose a name. Possibly, you will find, as I did, that someone in the profession is already using yours. I simply dispensed with Parsons and adopted Mim's maiden name – easy. The trick is not to go too far in trying to project this image or that. It's a great mistake to put all your eggs in one basket in this way. You will look bloody silly asking for a job at the Woolwich Tramshed if you've called yourself Barrington Courtenay.

Two christian names is the best combination; neutral, unintimidating and conveying to the director a reassuring sense of dependability. I wonder if we would have seen a second series of *To the Manor Born* if the leading lady's sage name had been Pip Trotsky. No, the people with the right idea are those who have opted for the two christian name format: Harriet Walter, Oliver Tobias, Anna Karen, Suzanne Danielle, Robert Lindsay, Paul Henry, Leslie Caron, Jonathan Cecil,

SIMON LE BON   WILLIAM JOB   BRIAN LOONEY

Remember! Once you've chosen it, you're stuck with it.

Robin Ray, Helen Cherry, Terence Alexander, Nigel Anthony, Christopher Benjamin, Alan Howard, Ann Lynn, Milicent Martin, Wendy Richard, Debbie Harry, Jane Seymour, Toni Arthur, June Barry, Susan George, Eleanor David, Lindsay Duncan, Peter Duncan and, if I may add my own name to this illustrious list, NICHOLAS CRAIG.

Of course, I would be absolutely mortified if any of these dear colleagues bought this book only because they're mentioned in it. I hope very much that they *will* buy the book, but for the right reasons.

Getting That Job

But anyway, how to get yourself started, that's the question. Well, it's tough. You needn't think that within two tenths of a second of your leaving drama school, hordes of stampeding directors are going to besiege you with offers of starring roles and bury you under a mountain of thousand-pound notes, because they won't. In fact, you might as well forget altogether about being a star, and if you have got it into your silly head that you are even remotely talented, well let me tell you, young sir or madam, that you aren't, and if you have any sense at all you will take yourself off to a remote rep and stay there for twelve years, by which time you should have learned to be a little less cocksure.

'OK,' you are probably saying, 'that's all very sound advice, but how do I, as a fledgling artist, a gosling on the duckpond of world theatre, how do I actually get a job?'

Right. As a beginner you can start by sending off a couple of dozen of these:

Dear ——————,
I am asking to inquire whether or not it would be at all feasible for you to spare some time in your most busy schedule to glance at the enclosed photograph and CV booklet with a view to possibly granting me the opportunity to give an albeit brief audition for you at your convenience at some point in the future.

I have recently learnt to juggle / play tabor / lute / drive H.G.V. / folk dance / basic scimitar.

Sorry to trouble you but I am at home in the following accents: Northern / Dover / King's Lynn / Continental.

Not too familiar, you see, and most important, not too clever-clever. After you have been going for a year or two, your status changes subtly, and it is then that you must take full advantage of any mutual contacts you may have with a director:

Dear ——————,
Another year has gone by and I realize that I haven't been in touch for yonks.

It's extraordinary to think that after all these years we've never actually met, but I know that, like me, you're an old mate of ——'s. And as I sat me down to pen this missive I bethought me, 'I wonder how he/she is.' Any news your end?

Anyway, I don't want to bore you any longer, so I'll just say that it would be smashing to work with you at long last.

The enclosed pic shows me with/without a beard but I can easily shave it off/grow one.

You can vary this according to circumstances, but it is important to maintain the light, bouncy, obedient tone of a good company member (GCM). However, a letter like the following will immediately brand you as a BCM (bad company member):

Dear ——————,
I would like to apply for an audition on 28th August, and would be grateful if you could let me know which plays you will be doing so that I may prepare an appropriate speech.
    Please return the enclosed photograph in the SAE provided.

Such presumptuous, self-important nonsense (this was a real letter believe it or not, shown to me by a director pal) will place you fairly and squarely beyond the pale rep-wise. A director is not some secretary whose sole function is to carry out your every instruction. He, or she, is an extremely important person who always wears the same clothes every day.

Finally, when you've knocked around the profession for a good few years, all the little cards and notelets you send to directors can have a much chattier tone:

Dear ——————,
How goes it with you then, you old bugger/ravishing creature? Christ, how long is it since we worked together? Yonkingtons. Any chance of a joblet?
    You owe me a drink, you rotten sod/fickle temptress. But seriously though, I'll buy you one.
    Not to nag, but if you happen to have a family solicitor or doctor or even a defending counsel sitting on your desk

with a question mark by their names, you might push one of them me-wards.

Anyway, better wend. You must come to dins one of these fine days.

But it will be a long time before you have acquired sufficient professional stature to use tricks like this.

Finding an Agent

I have never grovelled to anybody. Nevertheless there were times early in my career when it was necessary, shall we say, to 'perform' in ways not touched upon at drama school. I have no reason to be ashamed of this, nor did I at the time regard anything I did as humiliating, unhygienic or inhumane. It was simply good business.

The best time to look for an agent is, obviously, when you are in a play in London and your talents are there for all to see. Being in a play in the provinces is not so useful since agents rarely leave London for other than adulterous reasons.

I hasten to point out that I have the best agent in the world (Miriam) who is completely wonderful and a saint and to whom I am devoted. I would never dream of signing with any of the other agents who have offered to represent me and get me American TV work because I know that now she's nearly better and the office is redecorated she can hustle with the best of them, the lamb. When she puts her mind to it, she can be a very tough cookie indeed, which is exactly what I need because if it was up to me I'd just give in and say yes to anything. I'm hopeless.

Spotlight

The simplest way of advertising your wares (for what are we but humble hawkers in the bustling bazaar of Thespis Street?)

The Spotlight

MICHAEL JACQUES

Versatility – the greatest gift an actor can possess.

RODNEY BEWES

PETER CROUCH LTD.
5/6, COVENTRY STREET, W.1
01-734 2167/9

Props can add a nice humour touch.

JOHN HURT

PLUNKET GREENE LIMITED
118, Jermyn Street, St. James's Square, S.W.1
01-930 0811

Fashion is enormously important, of course.

Spotlight – *money well spent.*

is to advertise in the casting directory *Spotlight*. This will cost you about £130 and it is money well spent (though God knows, I haven't paid mine this year). It is vital to pick the right photo of yourself; remember, this is the one directors, producers and casting directors will be looking at for the next five years or so. It is very, very important that you look your best.

Equity

Equity is a trade union is a trade union is a trade union. Has to be, got to be, must be. It's unavoidable. Sorry, but there we are.

I'm pretty much of a middle-stump trade unionist, myself. Basically, I believe that anyone who has a burning desire to act (to be an actor) should be allowed, nay required, to join Equity, but not if he's just some yob who runs a string of launderettes in Leytonstone and is going to deprive real actors of small parts in *Minder* and *EastEnders*. If we let anybody in we might as well all go and work in a factory and have clocking-on cards because that is what it will be like.

All political parties and ideologies have some support within the membership of Equity. Once you have joined, you will have to affiliate yourself to one of the following pressure groups:

S.W.E.E.T.I.E. (Socialist Workers for Enforcing an End To Imperialist Enslavement)

L.U.V. (Lock Up Vanessa)

C.R.A.V.A.T. (Centre Right Actors Against Anarchist Trots)

S.O.P.P.I.E.S. (Silly Old Politics Prevents Important Engagements in South Africa) Not that I ever belonged to any of these groups, especially this one, and anyone who says I did is a liar and I'll sue them.

K.I.S.S. (Kill Imperialists, Smash Sexists)

C.U.D.D.L.E. (Chorus Understudies and Dressers Demand Longer Engagements)

Jobfacts

A few more facts and figures which may be of interest to the young actor

Casting Directors	Work no.	Home no.	Gift ideas
Doreen Bones	020 7387 1359	020 8982 8060	Dissecting equipment/ fluffy gonks
Irene Hunter	020 7261 4345	020 8750 6140	Snoopy ephemera/ raw offal
Esther Gore	020 7759 2388	020 8897 9761	Live poultry/ pink roses/ pre-war electrodes
Maud Charnel	01147 837 2452	01147 402 3261	New born babies/ dentists instruments

Acting Tips for Beginners

Hands

Your hands are your most expressive tools. Don't rush too quickly into deciding how you are going to use them. Carry your script and wear a big overcoat for most of the rehearsal period; then, when you are good and ready, you can opt for one of the positions shown opposite.

On no account must you mix styles. I remember a chaotic matinee at Stratford when Jim Olroyd, striving for emphasis, went to hook his thumbs into his waistcoat pocket only to bring his toga tumbling around his ankles.

Hands – Straight.

Hands – Comedy.

Telephone technique – the receiver should be held well away from the face.

Not in the mouth.

Keeping your end up

It has to be said that there are certain actresses who are apt to unbalance a play by getting all the laughs and generally drawing attention to themselves. I find that by moving slightly or making a noise every time they deliver a punchline, it is possible to pull the production back on to a more equal footing. Acting is about sharing.

Soldiering

There comes a point in any history play where guards are required to keep watch during a long meeting between military leaders. The rookie actor should always be ready to dodge out of the director's eyeline when it comes to staging these scenes. Think ahead. How much more pleasant to be watching *Newsnight* in the green room with a glass in your hand than to be up onstage glued to a spear or rifle for the whole of Act Four.

Corpsing

As all my friends will tell you, I am the worst, but I mean the very worst giggler. I remember the night when Bob Proudfoot did the whole of the Queen Mab speech with a Fergie mug in his liripipe – I was in utter fits and completely helpless. It is not an episode I am remotely proud of, because corpsing is very, very unprofessional; it is unfair to the other actors and disrespectful to the audience. There are a number of childish ways in which unprofessional actors will try to make one 'go up'. Beware.

Messages written on props or on your eyelids are basic ploys. Then there are live hamsters and 'doggie-do' novelties placed in desk drawers, rude pictures tucked into letters, a dildo in the fireplace, a condom on the end of spear, a Tiller Girl routine in the wings, superglue under the cucumber sandwiches, and – an old favourite of mine – simulated sex acts on the offstage side of a window. The upstage turn, of course, opens up a vast range of opportunities from funny faces to genital exposure.

So, yes, although corpsing is unprofessional, it would never do to acquire a reputation for being a non-giggler (N. G.), and there are times – for example, if a star actor tries, however feebly, to 'get' you – when it is unforgivably ill-mannered not to corpse.

Acting is essentially a question of teamwork.

Don't forget the Diva
Consideration towards backstage staff is something young actors often neglect. The pioneer of backstage philanthropy was the great Australian soprano, Nellie Melba. Melba was the first major performer to show practical concern for the well-being of stagehands It is said that, before a performance, she would invite as many as half a dozen of them into her dressing-room for a plate of something and a quick gulp. Many of today's leading actors continue this tradition. I will often 'treat' a crew myself. It is a pleasant distraction from pre-perf pressures to bring a smile to the 'techie's' face. Wardrobe mistresses, box-office staff, stage doormen, canteen ladies will all respond to a little individual attention.

Getting paid
It used to be common practice for some agents to keep their clients' fees until the actor came raging in to the office pleading starvation. Whereupon the books would be examined and, with a 'Hello, what's this?', the agent would find a record of payment. Salaries are passed on immediately nowadays, but repeat fees are still liable to do a stint in a W1 deposit account before reaching the actor.

But money doesn't actually mean very much to me to be quite honest. As long as I can buy my booze and fags and pay my mortgage and have a week or two on Lesbos and a Winterbreak and the odd din at L'Escargot, then I'm happy.

Dear me . . .
I have touched elsewhere on my fiercely analytical approach to a text, but I thought it might be instructive for the young actor to see the practical application of my methods. The following is an actual page from my *Cuckolde of Leicester* script:

THE CUCKOLD OF LEICESTER

Act 4/Sc. 7.

Props: sword
thongs
sweat

handwritten left margin: 3 black / 4 white / 1 tea with / 2 teas without

handwritten top right: O F C / T R A / H S R / CART/HRSOE / CARY HORES / CRAT SHORE / HAST ERROC — 348

MEDIOCHRITE: And if I cannot with my Truepate be,

No other lover shall these poor eyes see. 285

handwritten left: Wait till she screams, then run on.

(SHE BLINDS HERSELF AND EXITS DISTRESSED)

ENTER TRUEPATE AND PHILATIO DISGUISED

AS CAPUCHINS.

handwritten: up to pull vol · to · £10

TRUEPATE: Full fed am I upon the meal of exile,

handwritten left: WAVE ARMS ABOUT

And yet my hunger rages still for vengeance.

So like the Nubian eel that squirmeth in the mud, *handwritten:* Show legs

We come unseen, Philatio, into the fell Aldonzo's court.

handwritten: Hand on sword, finger pointing at willy.

PHILATIO: Full forty years it is since, like th'Athenian cat, my pads did tread 290

handwritten left: GET SWORD OUT. SEE A MOUSE. CHASE IT KILL IT. BLOW NOSE

these foul usurper's flags. And now, good Truepate, must you know that

I, your *(faithful)* friend Philatio, am in sooth your faithful *(loving)* cousin, Slype. When

thou was but a mewling chick, mine uncle Atrocitus, whom you thought was *handwritten:* Handstand here?

slain but lives, did pass you into Falseface's crib, and Falseface thence *handwritten:* cat

into Marcellus'. So, gentle friend that was and coz that is, I must 295

embrace thee twofold.

TRUEPATE: This news, like lampreys to a jaundiced friar, brings cruel joy. *handwritten:* Think of Jimmy Carter

For I am sworn to slay mine own uncle

If what you spake was true. *handwritten:* THINK HONOUR!

PHILATIO: As true as Jephtha's sow gives suck at Candlemas and then, 300

Being dry of dug, does make for Lincoln. *handwritten:* Jump about. Rostra etc...

TRUEPATE: Nor flames of hell nor Jupit's bolt can sway my purpose. *handwritten:* very loud.

handwritten left: quieter. Pull Tim dis.

But, monebantur, Aldonzo doth approach.

ENTER ALDONZO.

ALDONZO: Full four Septembers hath ten times bestrewn their golden burden

'Pon this kingdom ere I seized the crown. 305

handwritten: — pong this

TRUEPATE: Yet ere another poison'd leaf do fall

I mean to lop this usurping branch

And pulverize its putrid bark to pulp. *handwritten:* spray first 3 rows of audience with Sp...

ALDONZO: 'Pparel of Capuchin yet tongue of Malcontent's whore. Methinks it

handwritten left: Start screaming

is my hideously deformèd nephew Truepate. 310

TRUEPATE: Aye, 'tis Truepate. And Truepate comes, like old Enceladus, to squash

the worm Aldonzo and throw his cankerous carcase to the dogs i' the rialto.

handwritten: Draw sword. Grunt. · Remember he's your uncle.

ALDONZO: You are naughty, Truepate, and must perish in a sea of foaming gore.

THEY FIGHT *handwritten:* lunge-parry-turn-sweep-grunt-stagger- retreat-duck-charge and in.

TRUEPATE: Now, return, Aldonzo, usurping worm, to the sod that bore thee

foully up. HE SLAYS ALDONZO. 315

handwritten: BLOW, PANT, DROP SWORD; LEAN HEAD BACK TO FIND LIGHT THEN SLUMP.

The Theatre: Mythology and Superstition

With acting being such an incredibly dangerous, high-risk, kill-or-be-killed job, I suppose it is not surprising that there are superstitions and traditions relating to just about every stage of our working process. To the tyro board-treader, a rehearsal room on Day One is a veritable minefield. Solecisms and gaffes seem to come as easily as breathing to the greenhorn mirror of the times.

Everyone knows the old chestnuts like: never quote from the Scottish play, don't hop in the dressing-room and never wear green in Shaw, but there are many more no less revered superstitions, the flouting of which can cause terrible anguish to one's fellow actors.

Forewarned is forearmed.

Never wear your jazz pants to a readthrough; never call Sir Nigel Hawthorne 'Prickdust' during the first week of rehearsal – it drives him mad; never wear a monocle in that certain Norwegian play in which a particular lady shoots herself. If you have to do a sword fight, always carry a needle and thread in your pocket (this dates from the days when actors had to stitch up their own flesh wounds while they were performing). In fact many superstitions have common-sense, practical origins, the most obvious example being the old adage about never having crocodiles loose on stage.

Have you noticed how Anthony Hopkins often acts with his fists clenched? Well, he's got a rabbit's foot in each hand, that's why. And the famous Tony Sher sideways scuttle? – trying not to step on the cracks in between the boards, the superstitious old noddle.

And don't any of you try to tell me that there's nothing in these superstitions.

At Runcorn rep many years ago, I was sharing a dressing-room with several other actors. Some of us younger ones were larking about, hopping, quoting from the Norwegian play, cleaning silver and being generally scathing about theatrical superstitions. Now also in the dressing-room was an older actor, a rather shy and unobtrusive old chap, whom none of us really knew. He was deeply disturbed by our antics and, choking into his make-up box, he begged us to stop. 'Macbeth!' we shouted, and with all the cruelty of youth, we hopped with renewed vigour.

During that night's performance, the following things happened; one of my colleagues forgot to leave the bottom button of his waistcoat undone; I said, 'There's a train to Waterloo in half an hour,' instead of, 'There's a train to Waterloo *Station* in half an hour'; the rain in Act One was barely audible, which made nonsense of the line, 'Looks as though it's setting in. You'd better all stay the night here at the Manor.'

We returned to the dressing-room after the performance, shaken but still determined to show how sceptical we were. We whistled into the mirrors, put salt in our shoes and wore

The author at home on the South Bank. 'I walk absolutely every-where.'

That look!

our jerseys inside out, inviting the fates to strike us down. It was then that I noticed that my lighter had disappeared from my dressing table. I looked everywhere but there was no sign of it. Still more curiously, there was no sign of the old actor whom we had earlier offended. We looked for him in the pub and then at the digs without success. When he did not appear for rehearsals the following day, nor the next, even the most sceptical among us reluctantly had to admit that the old boy must have been a theatre ghost.

Twelve years later, I happened to be walking down Shaftesbury Avenue when who should I bump into but our old actor. He greeted me with great affection and congratulated me on my recent success. I was intrigued and I suppose I felt a little sorry for him, so I suggested we go for a drink in the Salisbury.

'So you weren't a ghost then,' I said, offering him a cigarette.

'A ghost?' he growled. 'Whatever made you think that?'

Then, as he moved to light our cigarettes, my jaw dropped. I couldn't believe my eyes.

There, in his hand, was a lighter which didn't remotely resemble the one I had lost.

'So you didn't take my lighter either?'

'My dear fellow, why should I have done that?'

'Well then, why did you leave so suddenly on that fateful night?'

'Got offered a commercial, old love. Never did like Runcorn much anyway.'

'I see,' I said, trying to piece it all together in my mind. 'What was the commercial for?'

'Matches,' he said, and my blood ran cold.

Which is why, from that day to this, I have never hopped, whistled, put salt in my shoes or worn a monocle in Isben. And if Peter Shaffer were to write me a play which had crocodiles in it I would have no option but to turn it down. (You could always use alligators, Peter.)

10

Crisis of Doubt

It was during the RSC's regional tour of The *Cuckolde of Leicester* that I had one of those experiences which make you wish you'd chosen a less dangerous way of earning a living – shark-wrestling perhaps, or bomb disposal. Although, in all honesty, I don't think I'd have made a success of either. I did go through a stage of wanting to be a doctor. I found the idea of healing people very, very exciting, still do, and indeed I like to think that, just as the physician heals the body, the actor heals the spirit. I'd have been no good at surgery, though. I'm spectacularly hopeless at anything remotely technical, quite inept, I'm afraid. So if you want a fuse mending or a shelf putting up then Craig is most definitely *not* your man. I'm a total disaster.

Anyway, for three months we had been touring the provinces (where the *real* people are, incidentally) performing in halls and community centres in places where the poor benighted tax payer is cruelly and senselessly denied the chance to see late-Jacobean tragedy performed on a thrust stage.

This particular week, we had set up our 'mobile theatre' in a sports centre in Loughborough. I was attempting to get into my Truepate costume in a singularly cold and cheerless changing-room normally used by referees. (I honestly don't know how these refs manage – one sixty-watt bulb, a cracked mirror, and then they get abused the moment they walk on to the pitch.) Anyway, somehow the slap (make-up) was going on – a monumental chore this (see page 155); wig, lashes, nose, beard, family wart and plenty of Leichner No.12 for anno domini. Slowly but surely, it was all coming together; some '14' on the nose, spot of '3' on the earlobes and a big dollop of '47' on the Adam's apple. In spite of the awful conditions, Truepate was beginning to 'live'.

I could hear the audience trickling into the gym next door, an exquisite moment of fear and pleasure. More pleasure on this occasion, since there was a party in from Mitsubushi, the firm sponsoring our week at Loughborough. There were only about twenty of them, but I knew that once we got to the disembowelment scene in Act Four, we'd have them eating out of our hands. Japanese audiences always love *The Cuck*.

I was just buckling on the leg-irons when I caught sight of myself in the mirror. I don't know how and I don't know why, but without any warning a terrible feeling of uselessness overcame me. It was like being struck by lightning. Dark, nightmare thoughts floated into my brain where before there had been none. Who was I helping? Who was I feeding? What would Bob Geldof say? It suddenly seemed as though *The Cuckolde of Leicester* was boring and incomprehensible. What was the point of doing it to twenty Mitsubushi reps? What was the point of doing it to anyone? I was sobbing uncontrollably, '5' streaming down my face. No way could I play Truepate in that state.

Several people must have heard my screams because soon the dressing-room was filled with anxious-looking actors in various states of undress. Bill Wackerbath, wearing nothing but his jock-strap and hump, was absolutely distraught. His face, I swear, had turned '53'. Bob Proud-foot had accidentally stubbed out a Number 6 on his chin, so he had a nasty burn. They were deeply concerned in the way that only actors can be when one of their number is in trouble. Fiona, our wondrous stage manager, was the first to ask what the matter was. It sounds awful now, but apparently I turned to them and said,

'God, I wish I'd done that *Bergerac* instead.'

'He's right, it's shite is this,' said big Jim Olroyd, ever the bluff Geordie. 'Let's fuck off back to the hotel.'

'Or we could go for a Chinese,' suggested Bob, for my black despair was spreading through the company like a cancer.

'I'm not going to that awful sloppy Cantonese place again,' said Harriet, the wise and beautiful.

But before the argument could develop, Fiona stated calmly but firmly, 'There may only be twenty Mitsubushi executives and their wives out there, but they have paid for a good night out.'

'We'd be doing the stupid twats a favour then,' said Jim, his Tyneside vowels swooping like swallows.

A compromise scheme was floated whereby, rather than doing all seven acts, we should just do the emotional curtain call at the end. I pointed out that, for me, this was the most exhausting part of the evening, and that we might as well do the whole play as just do that bit. So a vote was taken and the majority decision was that the cast should go to a restaurant, monopolize the place and generally show off. Like naughty schoolgirls, we tried to decide where to go in this strange and unfamiliar town.

'Come on, that Chinese place wasn't too bad,' said Bob.

'No, Darling,' said Harriet, 'if you want eight pound forty's worth of washing-up water it's ideal.'

It had become frighteningly clear that the cast was now so racked with self-doubt that the future of the tour, indeed of the RSC itself, was in grave danger. Certainly as far as tonight was concerned, a *Cuck* was out of the question.

By now Bob had produced a *Good Food Guide* and was looking up Loughborough. To everyone's disappointment, there wasn't a single entry. But somehow their mad talk stirred something in my soul. Through that funny little dressing-room floor, I felt weird vibrations – the voices of the actors down the ages talking to me through my toes; Roscius, Burbage, Garrick,

1.43 p.m. The blank canvas.

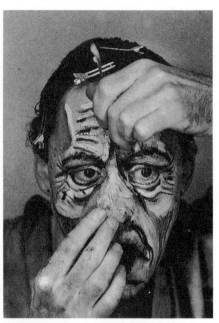

2.15 p.m. Sketching the nuances.
Detail is all.

3.30 p.m. Only four hours to go. I
begin to feel the first labour pains.

4.45 p.m. I'm on the runway. No
turning back now. Bloody hell!

6.03 p.m. My agent calls. Apparently
there is still a world out there!

7.12 p.m. Truepate is born. However, it is immensely important to switch off for a few minutes pre-perf.

Peter Barkworth, commanding me, through my feet, to lead my fellow actors to the stage. 'Act. Act. Act,' they chorused (the ancients are usually right, I've found). 'Act. Act. Act. O acta Nicholus!'

'Look,' I said, 'we are actors, we are gipsies, we are mirrors of the times. We have an immense responsibility, and an enormous – an immense – duty to the public, and everyone. And a tremendous . . .'

I don't recall exactly what else I said and, in fact, Harriet interrupted me before I had properly finished.

'Look, Darling,' she said, 'if we can't find anywhere decent to eat then, quite honestly, we might as well do the fucking show.'

'We are special people,' I said. 'Immensely special.' Looking around me, I knew that I had swung the mood of the dressing-room. Where, before, there had been fourteen actors discussing Chinese restaurants, I now saw a powerful, humming acting-machine just aching to get its corporate laughing gear round seven acts of late-Jacobean blank verse.

'We have an enormous gift. Immensely so. A tremendous...' Even as I spoke the dressing-room started to empty, these wonderful, magical actors knowing in their hearts that they must return to prepare for their various roles. For the dolorous, strangely hypnotic rhythms of the dear old *Cuck* are more satisfying than any quantity of bean-curd and abalone. A quaint old-fashioned quality called dedication had won the day. It just so happened that it had fallen to me single-handedly to avert disaster.

As I leapt on to the stage to deliver my first speech, not a single Mitsubushi rep – or his lady wife – could have had an inkling of the near catastrophe which had taken place.

'Aaaarrrggghhh!' I began. 'For sixteen years Aleppo was mine gaol / Now would I most bloodily avenged be.'

Bullseye! I could always tell from the way that first line came out whether or not *The Cuck* was going to fly. That night it had condor's wings. They were hungry, this audience, hungry for *The Cuck*, hungry for Truepate. And, yes, it occurred to me I was feeding them. That was why I was there. That was why I was an actor. That was why I was so enormously important. That was why I had devoted the whole of my life to the theatre. Geldof can 'Feed the World' but he can't feed Mitsubushi. Only I can do that. Only me. Only I, AN ACTOR.

Do it!

Stern and bulbous stand the wig-blocks,
Harsh the spirit gum.
Putty in the make-up box,
For noses yet to come.

A bank of telemessages,
A furry pig from Sue,
A plate of curling sandwiches,
Chrysanths from 'You know who!'

And it's out through the door at 'Beginners Please',
And it's 'Good luck, Bill' and it's trembling knees,
And it's down the dark stairs to the wings to wait,
And it's fear and big hugs – and a minute to eight!

Oh when will it end, this exquisite pain?
When can we all do kissing again?
Then the voice of a dresser rallies the ranks,
'Did you get my card? Got a fag? Ooh, thanks.'

Oh why must we work in those freezing church halls?
Why do we suffer those ten o'clock calls?
Why do I sweat in an inch of Max Factor?
Because, matey, you're a bloody good actor.

11

Envoi

Since writing the last chapter, an extraordinary thing has happened to me. I was lying in the bath last week reflecting on the paradoxical fact that certain publishers insist on ringing one up at unearthly hours of the morning demanding manuscripts despite the fact that they were told very clearly that one was completely hopeless about deadlines. Ho-hum.

Anyway, as I say, the phone rang. Miriam.

'Prepare yourself for a shock, Darling. The Americans want you for a new television series.'

Well, I wasn't very enthusiastic, I'm afraid, and merely made some rather grumpy enquiries about what and when and where. It appeared that the series was to be about a rich family who owned a string of hotels, and mine was to be a running character.

'They want you to fly out to L.A. in a fortnight, Darling.'

'Impossible. I'm doing a *MacTavish* at Rickmansworth W.I. on the 6th and another one at Hatfield House on the 27th.'

'Yes, but . . .' said Miriam, and I listened while she told me all about it. All the usual guff: they desperately wanted me; I was the most compelling actor of my generation – the award proved that; if they wanted just another competent English performance they'd have asked for Jeremy or Charles or even, at a pinch, Anthony, but no, they wanted Craig. My initial response was, as you can imagine, 'Thank you but – yawn –

boring – don't want to know – rather do something nice in The Pit.'

'Yes, I know,' said Miriam. 'I know how we feel about telly and America and everything, but there's something I think you ought to know.'

Well, she told me – and my jaw dropped a mile. Then I thought I must have misheard her, so I asked her to repeat it. Down went the Craig jaw again. I simply couldn't believe it – they were offering me *the* most phenomenal amount of scope to develop the character. A new assistant manager comes to the hotel and has some rather fuddy-duddy English ideas about how things should be run. It seemed to me to be saying one hell of a lot about how, despite sharing a common language, people on either side of the Atlantic frequently misunderstand one another. And there were some nice little humour touches as well. I had to play him.

American television is very much aimed at the popular market and, as someone who sees himself very much as a communicator, I applaud that, a lot. I cannot understand this English aversion to anything which is popular. In fact, let's face it, the English hate success, don't they? It all just seems a little bit silly to me. Envy is at the root of it of course.

So, in two days I'm off. Farewell then, little Richmond house; bye-bye, garden; adieu, my collection of Victorian chamber-pots; auf wiedersehen, epic walks across London; au revoir, those lovely dins at L'Escargot; big hugs, Bill and Bob and dear mad Hat; à bientot, beloved Nash and Barbican; pip-pip, Shaftesbury Ave; chin-chin, make-up box – we've had some times, eh?; napoo, nose putty; sayonara, my Thursday night K'Dang classes; goodbye now, Radio Four; goodbye, draughty old rehearsal room; goodbye, Theatre and goodbye, dear, gentle, patient reader, you were wonderful. I love you.

Glossary of Theatrical Terms and Expressions

Agent – (n) Failed actor

A.S.M. – (n) A trifler with married actors' affections. Liable to make unrealistic demands at the end of a tour.

Assistant Director – (n) Young graduate of good birth and private means.

Audition technique – (phr) Unnatural sexual activity.

Barbican bunk-up – (phr) Masturbation.

BBC – (n) Exclusive West London luncheon club (no ties allowed).

Berk off – (v. vulg) To go to Los Angeles.

Biggy – (n) Large part.

Big hugs – (phr) Formal greeting.

Billington – (n) A pun, so uproariously funny that whole paragraphs have to be specially written in order to accommodate it.

Bizden – (pub) *The Stage Yearbook* (published annually).

Bogarde – (v) To monopolize a film (Sixties slang).

Book of 'Job' – (phr) *The Spotlight* Directory in which actors advertise under the following sections:

Juvenile: (middle-aged actors)
Juvenile Character: (ugly middle-aged actors)
Leading: (older actors unable to do accents)
Character: (very old, ugly actors. Can do some accents)
Children and Younger: (all other actors).

Bowles – (n) (tailoring term) Large shoulder pads, e.g. 'Look at the *Bowles* on that jacket.'

Callow – (v) To expose one's genitals for dramatic effect.

Camping about – (phr) Pre-performance relaxation technique.

Canteen neck – (cond) An unpleasant stiffness caused by continuous turning of the head, c.f. Club crick.

Cast me – (n) A small office sofa.

Chadwick Street, to be in – (v) To be unemployed. Also: sausage, not a; pipeline, nothing in the; point, what's the fucking?

Cottesloe knee – (cond) Inflammation caused by acting on all fours.

Critic – (n) Failed playwright.

C.V. – (n) Unpublished autobiography, written in the form of a Victorian three-volume novel.

Drama teacher – (n) Failed director.

Enjoy – (v) To make a desperate attempt to save a doomed production, e.g. Director: 'Just enjoy it, loves.'

Farce bandit – (n) An accomplished and elegant light comedian.

Friend of Trevor's, a – (n) An eminent classical actor (must be able to sing and dance).

Go on tour, to – (v) To commit adultery.

Grant – (n) An unnecessary stammer at the start of a sentence. Can extend a scene substantially.

Indisposed – (adj) Hopelessly drunk.

Laertes' elbow – (cond) Caused by playing a character who has a two-hour break in the middle of the play. Symptoms: unsteady legs, slurred speech.

'Laugh? I nearly forgot my agent's birthday!' – (exp) I was highly amused.

Perf – (n abbr) Performance.

Playwright – (n) Complete idiot. Usually good for a drink.

Producer – (n) Failed director, but with private means.

Profesh – (n abbr) Our wonderful calling.

Royal National Theatre – (n) Heritage centre dedicated to the golden age of the American musical.

Sinden – (n) Formally structured theatrical anecdote ending with the sentence, 'Amazingly, the audience were entirely unaware of anything amiss!'

Talented – (adj) Critic's euphemism for actors of non-caucasian ethnic origin. 'This talented cast . . .'

Wonderful – (adj) First night term describing sub-standard perf. Also; bored for a moment, I wasn't; old bugger, you've done it again, you.

Steven Spielberg takes a box at the Royal Court, 1980.

Acknowledgements

Well, I've done it. It's taken time but I've done it.

Writing *I, An Actor* has been an expedition for me, an intellectual journey to the land of self-knowledge. That the journey was completed has been largely due to my two sturdy pack animals, Christopher Douglas and Nigel Planer. Brought in to help only a few months ago, they have cajoled me when my concentration has wandered and restrained me when my pen has run away with itself. They have borne my reminders that the carpet is not an ashtray and that the Wine Society's Rioja does not grow on trees with good heart. Thanks boys.

Essentially, writing a book is the same as producing a play. Your early notes and rough drafts are your rehearsals, your author is your cast, your launch party is your first night and the guests your audience – even though they don't actually read the book until afterwards. Of course, there is no performance per se, and you don't have a curtain or anything, but there is lots and lots of white wine and picky bits just like at a first night party. And people *do* take photographs.

Above all, it's teamwork. None of it could happen without the back-room girls and boys, and it is to them that I dedicate this, my debut on the literary stage.

First and foremost must come my lovely photographer, Nobby Clark (such a delightful name, I forbid you to change it to something less old-fashioned). Snapping at his heels (as well as some of his most valued clients) are Chalky Whyte, John

Timbers, Trevor Leighton, Michael Barnett and Han Lee de Boer.

I must also thank Helen Ewing, who designed the book – or rather had lots of clever ideas and then ended up doing exactly what I suggested in the first place. (Funny, isn't it, how time and time again, one has to do everything oneself?)

Thank you, darling Gerald Scarfe (whom I suspect I helped out of a little bit of a hole by commissioning the cartoon).

I would like to say a great big sloppy thank you to Max Eilenberg and his smashing crew at Methuen but it would be entirely inappropriate after the way I've been treated. A bit of a mish-mash indeed.

I am indebted to Andrew Nickolds for sniffing out two such clever young men to help me.

I would like to thank Phoebe Scholfield, my Girl Friday, and a game little actress in her own right, bless her.

I would like to send big hugs to Peter James and his team of embattled poppets down at the Lyric Hammersmith.

I would like to thank my costume designer, Frances Haggett, and my make-up artiste, Jan Harrison-Shell. Also Steven O'Donnell, Robert Kirby and Mark Lucas, even though they are always sending me up, the evil buggers.

A special kiss to Mickey Gambon for lending me his dressing-room and water pistol.

I would like to thank my greatest fan, Roy Moseley – a sweet chap and a peerless kitchen-tidier – for going through the files and hunting out the photo of me as a nipper.

Finally, I would like to thank the greatest Darling of them all, the One without whom none of this would have been possible – my Mother. Dearest Mim.

Actavi – I have acted. Now for a pint.

Postscript to the 2001 Edition

An actor should always heed the advice of his agent. With her experience, expertise and professional good judgement, it is the agent rather than the silly emotional actor who is in the better position to make important career choices. Sorry, I forgot to introduce myself – I'm the Queen of Sheba.

I did indeed go to America on Miriam's advice to appear in the aforementioned TV series, *Hotel Intercontinental*. I did indeed attempt to inhabit the psyche, walk in the shoes and get behind the retina of the Berkeley Savoy character. And I can reveal to you now, as I did to Miriam at the time, that it was a complete and utter total waste of time and that the United States television industry is quite the seediest, dumbest most unprofessional medium I have ever had the misfortune to act in; that its bejewelled, bearded executives are as brainless as they are sockless and illiterate; that its workforce is as obese as it is ignorant, and that their collective sense of taste extends no further than an ability to distinguish between different kinds of melted cheese. I said all this to Miriam, though in rather more robust terms than would be appropriate here. I can safely say that no one was more relieved than me when the *Hotel Intercontinental* writers decided to have Berkeley Savoy fall down the lift shaft and die in Episode 2. Fortunately I was one of the few people working on the programme that was physically capable of fitting into a lift; otherwise I might still be out there. Never have I been so thankful to get out of a job in my life.

I've long since forgiven Miriam for landing me in it but I hope she understands why some of our conversations ever since have been tinged with a smidgeon of scepticism on my part.

As I have written in the introduction to this new edition, the years following my return from America brought innumerable pinnacles and resplendent accolades of which one can be inordinately proud, but perhaps the most lustrous achievement of all is simply to have survived thus far. That, after all, is something that cannot be said of all the actors mentioned in the preceding pages. So one likes to think one has achieved a certain status in the profession, although you'd never know it from the way I've been treated sometimes.

When one looks back over a long career, it is all too easy to concentrate only on the peaks and plateaus and to overlook the troughs of despair, humiliation and downright treachery that lie between. These are the real chronicles of an actor's life; the rubble of disappointment and shards of shattered hopes, the broken promises, the insulting radio fees, the inefficient publishers, the showers that don't work, the endless begging letters from students wanting you to pay their drama school fees, the bonkers bloody autograph hunters, the voice-over directors who keep wanting you to 'do it again but a bit more like Stephen Fry' and, oh, those *countless, POINTLESS* meetings at BBC Television Centre where they make you sit in Reception for half a day before the self-satisfied little twelve-year-old prig of a producer, with his laminated ID flapping on the lapel of his horrid *Next* jacket, actually deigns to come down and say what an honour it is to meet you and that the part has been specially written with you in mind – oh yeah, in that case why is Piggott-Smith sitting on the other side of Reception with a copy of the same bloody script in his hands?

Then there was the sitcom going down the tubes. You just can't believe a single word anyone says these days. They are criminals basically.

Which is why, when one's agent makes certain remarks about it being very tough out there these days, I tend to reply that I do not need to be told how tough it is – I am the one who is out there experiencing the aforesaid fucking toughness. What I need from you, Miriam, is not lectures on the state of the business but a bit of support. Which you do try to give, I know, and I appreciate it. I do. And I know you can't produce the kind of work I want out of a hat. It's just that sometimes the prospect of having to drag these tired old tits out on tour *again* is just too bloody depressing for words. Then I have another couple of gins and, of course, I start thinking, oh why not?

I think the problem really is that I'm just too trusting, too good-natured – naïve even. I seem to have this pathological inability to learn from experience.

But then if ninety-nine percent of your experiences are bad ones, what can you do? Lie in bed and never do anything ever again, I suppose.

But you would have thought, wouldn't you, that after the *Hotel Intercontinental* debacle if anyone had suggested a return to the land of the lardypants I would have run a mile. Oh dearie no sirree Bob. This is Muggins Craig we are talking about – you know, the one who gets a raw deal then goes straight back to the end of the queue and shuffles along holding his tray out for another helping of shit cassoulet.

So naturally the next time an opportunity arose to get on a plane, contort my knees into position either side of my chin and fly across the Atlantic to the land of Buzz Butterball, my response was 'Oh, yes please, I'd love to.' Woof woof, pant, pant, good doggie Nicholas, pat, pat, pat. I really do think it's getting to the point where they'll have to lock me up.

It was the lure of working with Peter and Edward Hall that did it. I was seduced really. Believe it or not, being asked to play the title role in John Barton's *Tantalus* seemed like an honour at the time. In fact, things went fine for the first year of rehearsal in Denver – we didn't hit turbulence until the week before we opened when suddenly the vastly experienced master Edward Hall announced that he wanted me to do 'much less wailing and stamping'. I mean, it's a Greek tragedy for goodness sake, not Noël flipping Coward. Then Peter suddenly told me I had to wear a mask. Well I'm sorry but the audience do not pay $200 a head to come and see their favourite actor only to find he's got a bloody mask on. And with the greatest respect, if Tantalus is Zeus's son – what's he doing hiding in a little corner downstage left like a mouse, IN A MASK, while Greg Hicks strides about with blood smeared all over his buttocks? I mean if anyone is going to occupy a central position with blood on his bottom then surely it should be Tantalus, unless of course the object of the exercise is to thoroughly confuse the audience, which wouldn't be very sensible as, let's face it, they aren't the brightest over there – it's a struggle at the best of times to distract them from fretting over where their next pile of giant pancakes is coming from.

Suffice it to say words were exchanged in *Starbucks* (not one syllable of which would I wish to retract, incidentally, although I would be prepared to meet a proportion of Peter's dry cleaning costs as I know maple syrup is a bugger to get out of cashmere.)

The upshot was that Peter and Edward then set about butchering John's masterly text with such barbarity that I felt unable to continue in the production. It's true that most of the scenes they cut were the ones in which I appeared so, in fact, there wouldn't have been much point in my turning up at the theatre anyway, but I would have pulled out in any event. Sometimes you have to just walk away and move on. Life, unlike *Tantalus*, is just too short. John Barton withdrew his labour in solidarity. He couldn't possibly have attached his name to a production whose leading character fails to make a single appearance in thirteen hours. It would have made John look ridiculous.

So there you are, you see. Craig once again treated as a fucking punch bag. I sometimes think directors, managements and producers see me and say, 'Ooh quick, there he is. How can we make his life a total misery?' To be honest one just gets so messed around these days that you actually come to expect it.

It's the same with publishers. As any reader who has followed me this far will know, I spent a nightmare year being buggered about by a team of incompetents who couldn't even get a simple book into the best seller charts, let alone organise a launch party that anyone who is at all jolly would remotely want to attend, but sure enough thirteen years later I can't wait to sign up with another mob who, if you can believe it, have just suggested doing without a launch party altogether. Then when you come up with a modest compromise like the Ivy, do they bother to furnish you with a civil response to your telephone call? Not since Bridget fucking Jones has validated their trivial existences they don't.

Oh and get this. Caroline Jolly Fucking Hockey Sticks from the Olivier Awards rang up to ask me would I present the award for Most Promising Newcomer. 'Delighted to. Great honour etc. Just give me the date, tell me the seating plan and fax over the menu.' It means I have to ask the Comic Relief office if I can possibly fly out to Malawi a day later but they're fine about that.

So far, so good.

It's now that the Olivier organisers cotton on to the fact that they are not dealing with an ordinary actor to whom a modicum of common courtesy might be due but Muggins McDoormat Craig. So Jemima Hockey Sticks rings again. 'Would you terribly mind presenting the award for the Most Promising Sound Design instead?' And the reason? (True story this.) Because some fucking yank sitcom rent boy is in town and they think it would be smashing if he handed over the

Newcomer Award instead of me, and was I cool about that?

I informed her that, alas, I was very far from cool about it and that she might care to consider shoving the fucking Sound Effects Award right up Mr Sitcom's fat American arse – not that he'd be likely to feel anything, from what I've heard about his habits. Phone down.

Ring ring. Is it Jemima Puddleduck calling back to apologise? Not a bit of it. It's Araminta Badminton-Horse-Trials from Comic Relief come to join the anti-Craig lynch mob.

'Nicholas, since you can't leave for Malawi on the day we originally wanted, okay, we wondered if – '

'No, it's all right, I can do it now.'

'But we thought, okay, instead of doing the piece standing by the well with Harry Enfield –'

'But I can go to Malawi.'

'Yes but we thought it'd be great, okay, if you did a piece with Ronnie Corbett in a community centre on the outskirts of Ebbw Vale, okay –'

'I am telling you, I am free to go to Malawi!'

'That's a real shame, okay, cause we've got the Pub Landlord instead now. So is that okay then?'

'No, dear, it is not fucking okay – okay? And I'll tell you why not. It is not okay because for thirty years I have been buggered up, pissed about and generally shat on by organisations like yours and I have quite simply had enough. OKAY? So you and Harry Enfield and Ronnie Corbett and the Pub Landlord and the BBC and Lord Olivier and those greedy fucking Malawians can fuck right off because you are all a bunch of fucking c***s and I hope you fall down your fucking well and fucking well drown . . .'

TAPE BECOMES INDISTINCT HERE.